UNDERSTANDING AND USING TIME

DR. VON GOODLOE

Copyright © 2025 VON GOODLOE
All rights reserved.
Printed in The United States.
ISBN 979-8-218-94058-4

ACKNOWLEDGMENTS

Writing this book has been a journey that I could never have completed alone. I owe my deepest gratitude to the many people who have offered guidance, support, and inspiration along the way. First and foremost, I would like to thank my family.

To my parents, who instilled in me a love of learning from a young age — your encouragement made this possible. To my partner, spouse and friend Sharon, thank you for your endless patience, and belief in me even when I doubted myself.

My sincere appreciation goes to my editor, Christy and my sister Beblon whose sharp insights and steady hand helped shape this book into its final form. Thanks also to my friends, Carey and Bobby for championing this project from the very beginning and insisting I start and complete it.
I am grateful to my friends and early readers Sharon, Sam, Beblon, Christy et al. for offering honest feedback, laughter, and motivation when I needed it most. You helped me see what this book could become.

Finally, I want to thank you, the reader. Your time and imagination bring these words to life. I hope this book gives you something meaningful in return. Remember always the time we are given is a gift, use it well.

With gratitude,

Von

CONTENTS

Preface

Chapter 1	Compartmentalization
Chapter 2	Stacking and Packaging
Chapter 3	Time Robbers
Chapter 4	Procrastination
Chapter 5	Conquering Worry
Chapter 6	Zero Talent
Chapter 7	Exercise and Being Idle
Chapter 8	Post Traumatic Stress Disorder and Time
Chapter 9	P5
Chapter 10	The Dreaded Meeting
Chapter 11	The Purpose of Time Management
Chapter 12	The Mindset of Time Management
Chapter 13	Motivation and Time Management
Chapter 14	Time Management Methodology
Chapter 15	Sharing Your Time with Others
Chapter 16	How Utilizing Proper Listening Techniques Can Impact Your Use of Time

Chapter 17	Managing How You Interact with Others
Chapter 18	Generational Differences and Their Effect on Your Usage of Time
Chapter 19	Rest and Wasting Time There is No Correlation
Chapter 20	Forgiveness and Time Management
Chapter 21	Practice Stress Reduction Techniques
Chapter 22	Setting Boundaries
Chapter 23	Recognize That You Are Telling a Story That Can Be Changed
Chapter 24	Decide
Chapter 25	Thankfulness and Other Personal Ideas…
Chapter 26	Race Ethnicity, Gender, and Sexual Orientation and use of Time
Chapter 27	Fluidity of Time
Chapter 28	The "To Do List" and Time Management
Chapter 29	Time and Specific Creations/Constructions
Chapter 30	Time Management Quotes
Chapter 31	Concluding Thoughts

References

About the Author

PREFACE

We are living in an era where time is of the essence and using it properly is not only necessary but essential. The question is, how do you know that you have time? Did you know that you have sold a portion of your time (life) to someone, or an entity? Our mindset concerning time can be so basic that by the time you realize that you are wasting it, you cannot get it back. This book contains basic and essential information to help your time on earth be happy, healthy, and meaningful. Since we know we did not create time, nor can we get it back after we have used it; we should consider based on order of importance, how we are going to use it, preserve it, and lastly utilize it properly for as long as possible.

Understanding and Using Time is a perfect way for those who have not considered nor are unbeknownst to them, to realize the importance of the gift that time is. An in-depth and considerate expanse of appreciation for the stretch that the author has dedicated to the intention of ensuring that from his own experience; how important and critical time is to living a productive, fulfilling, and exploratory life.

The author qualifies himself for the contents of each chapter from life's experiences spending thirty-six years of his life on a job with perfect attendance which means that a Fortune 500 corporation purchased his time for five days out of a week and eight or more hours each day! Only one with a vivid and positive imagination about being successful combined with determination and grit could make this happen today as the world continues in the utter confusion that exists.

Surely, we can conclude that there is evidence of life's purpose in all chapters of this book. Surprisingly, the context of the author's information over the years derived from daily conversations with others, meetings, observations, and the life experiences of others also, that inspired the writing of this book. All with the intention of life preservation and the fulfillment of abundant living because of understanding how to manage time and utilizing it as a basic and essential need for living just like the air you breathe.

Chapter: 1

Compartmentalization

The biggest barrier to most people's success in life is not intelligence, education, drive, relationships, or where they were born in the hierarchy of life; it is the proper use of time. Time is the only commodity that we have no idea of how much of it we have, can never create more of, and waste more than anything else.

Let us consider that humans start off in a hole regarding time. You may ask what do I mean by this? Essentially, for an average human being to function properly they need between 6-8 hours of sleep, this means we as humans can spend as much as one fourth of our existence unconscious and 75% of the time remaining for all other actions and activities. An average person works 8 hours a day, some more, some less. Let us say they are employed by someone who has made use of that 8-hour increment of their time; again, approximately 25% of that available time you had has been allocated to someone or something else, leaving 50% of the remaining time for other pursuits. The question is how will you manage the remainder of that time, and whether the percentages do or do not apply to you up or down, how will you use them to your advantage; or keep them from being a disadvantage?

Considering the advent of one of the greatest and most damaging technological advances in the modern era, the smart phone and associated similar devices, the average adult spends 4.2 hours per day on apps installed on their cellular device(s), that's almost 64 days a year. So, where are we now? We had 50% of our time remaining of the 24 hours a day left to be productive, or 12 hours and we dedicated 4 of these hours to our devices. As a result, there are, 8 hours left to be either productive, use for personal interaction with others, growth, reflection, introspection, planning, or action…the point is made.

Now I cannot say that all the 4.2 hours a day or 64 days a year is unproductive time. Only you, the reader, can judge for yourself as to what you consider how that time will be allocated. It is quite possible that not all the 4.2 hours a day

App use is unproductive on our devices. You may be paying bills, reading self-help literature, work related emails or being entertained by watching goat yoga, cats play a piano, or a man set his mouth on fire with burning hot chilies and running around a truck.

So, let us get back to the remaining 8 hours a day. If our supposition is correct and can be quantified scientifically and factually, how do high achieving individuals achieve amazing results using only 8 hours of available time a day?

This is what we will explore in this book. I have never considered myself a highly performing individual or an expert in time management, but I have been encouraged by a friend to share parts of my life in the hope that it aids others, he thinks it will. I have no idea if it will or not, but I will endeavor at least to make it an entertaining read. One thing I am aware of that will assist everyone, even if you read no further into this tryst, is that it is important to try to learn to compartmentalize so that your thoughts in one area do not compromise your activities in another area. How many times have

"Nothing Is as sad as wasted potential"

you been upset with your wife, girlfriend, husband, boyfriend or significant other and it has completely derailed your ability to complete a project, task or even something simple you planned to do? For most of us, the answer is probably, "lots of times". I am not saying do not deal with it. What I am really saying is deal with the issue, if possible. If you know you are wrong, apologize. If you know you are right, try to see other people's point of view. It might change or enhance your understanding or at least calm you down. Try to talk through the issue or concern, if possible and if you cannot, agree to disagree knowing that you tried. Make a promise or pact to try again later, with less friction. At this point this issue is not closed, but for some it can be placed in a holding container that I call a compartment to be fully dealt with later. This frees most, not all your mind, to work on another task, less important maybe, but something that still needs to be accomplished. This does not happen easily because human nature causes us to enjoy wallowing in our unhappiness instead of facing the issues that are causing them and working

"Nothing Is as sad as wasted potential"

towards solutions. The other cardinal sin we are guilty of is blaming others without looking at our contribution to the existing situation. I worked in Labor Relations for more than 20 years and I have rarely seen a situation where one side tells the story, then, the other side tells the story, and both stories are the same. Usually, the truth is somewhere in the middle. Not always, but many times it is. How is it that the only people witnessing a situation can see, feel, and experience it so differently that their recollection of events can often be diametrically opposed? I would be hazardous to say because in times of high stress, we view the world and all events mostly from only our own perspective to the exclusion of all others. This is like the work which has been done over and over where a simple story is told at one end of a room, and the facilitator asks the group to share the story with the next person and the next and the next and by the end of the line the story has completely changed. Our minds tend to recreate events based on our experiences, education and understanding. You must take extreme care when using this strategy because

"Nothing Is as sad as wasted potential"

to a loved one or a co-worker it can be perceived that you do not care or are not paying them adequate attention. Therefore, I request that you start by trying your best to assess your part in the issues and right or wrong, try your best to understand the other person's viewpoint and give the conversation a try if it does not become volatile. Try to stop thinking of situations in relationships as wars that need to be won or lost. Men are great at winning battles, but we rarely win the wars. Women know our buttons much too well. Winning a battle or a war of words at work and at home is usually a loss for both parties and results in hurtful feelings, separation, anxiety, and other issues to bring up in a later conversation to hurt the other person or derail the discussion.

Considering the diagram on the next page, each item is an issue that an average adult may be dealing with at any point in time in their life. Some of us even deal with all of them at once. Which one takes priority and for how long and does it taking priority keep you from devoting proper attention to another important item in another box? Some theorists would say now is

"Nothing Is as sad as wasted potential"

the time to place a value of importance on the A-Z or 1-10 etc. but when you start to think about these things, they are so intertwined that separating them begins to diminish the others. Compartmentalization says they are all important and must be dealt with but each in their own time with 100 percent focus and attention. The misconception that humans are great at multi-tasking comes from the fact that the brain is so complex and such a great machine that it can move from one task to the other with such velocity it seems as if we are multitasking. The mind is concentrating on one task then another, then another, then another and then another: similarly, a computer juggles information. The only difference is, the computer usually does not forget information and the human brain probably doesn't either, but we do lose access to information which results in the same thing. The brain stores things based on usage and need for recall. That is why a stupid jingle you hear a lot gets stuck in your head but a phone number you need to remember you just cannot quite recall.

"Nothing Is as sad as wasted potential"

UNDERSTANDING AND USING TIME

Consider the diagram below, each box is an issue an average person might be considering at any moment in time:

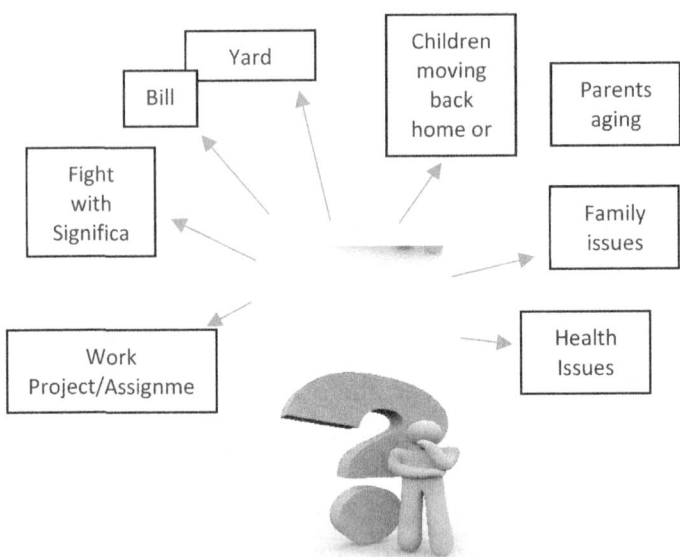

"Nothing Is as sad as wasted potential"

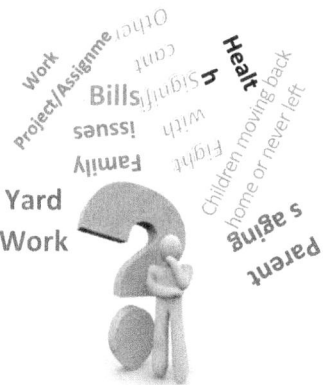

So, referencing the above diagram, most of us would like to believe that our thoughts are simple and organized like the above and we can sort through each concern as we need to and resolve them as time permits. The reality for most of us is most likely like the diagram below. A jumble of thoughts and a mishmash of levels of importance vying for the frontal lobe of our brain for action. Add to the fact that we may also be driving a car while listening to the radio, talking on our cell phone and for a few putting on makeup and eating some fries. No wonder there are so many accidents where a

"Nothing Is as sad as wasted potential"

person says I have no idea what happened, or they just pulled right out in front of me. Where was our attention really? If it were not for the capacity of our brain to process so much information so incredibly fast, I imagine there would be a thousand more accidents and incidents each day.

"Nothing Is as sad as wasted potential"

Chapter: 2
Stacking and Packaging

The next tool that I use I like to call "stacking or packaging". This is much different from the concept of multitasking. With stacking and packaging you take items on your list of need to do, want to do and must do then see if they can be combined or layered so that they can be completed concurrently. Many stay-at-home parents and mothers were/are champions of this. They can wash the clothes, clean the house, get the kids ready for school, check homework, cook breakfast and get themselves ready for work seemingly at the same time. This is because these activities have the characteristic of being packable.

When considering which activities to add to the stacking or packaging method, it is best to use activities that have what we will call dead time involved in their completion, and package them with time definite or activities that are conducive to start and stops.

Take for example washing and drying clothes. This is a much-needed activity in many households and one that is not really enjoyed. When I mentioned dead time, I mean once you start the activity in this example, the washing or drying cycle for a load along with having all the clothes sorted into appropriate piles, there is unused or dead time until the cycle ends, and the clothes can be moved to the next step in the process. After a few uses of any washer or dryer most people can gauge how much time is available between movement either to the dryer or another part of the process. This time, whether it is an hour or 30 minutes, can be used to complete another item in another compartment that only needs up to an hour to complete. This might be anything from loading the dishwasher and/or cleaning the kitchen or doing an hour of yard work or ironing clothes that have already been through the complete cycle. You could also use this time to check and respond to necessary emails or any other mundane activity or chore that requires the amount of time available.

Using this stacking and packaging methodology, to complete tasks for multiple activities that require rote memory, but not necessarily large amounts of brain power, can be completed easily. The result is clearing multiple compartments in a smaller amount of time and freeing up time to deal with items in other compartments later.

As items are completed using this method, tasks that individually could take up a full day can be managed down to a quarter or less of the total time used of your day. The wonderful thing about this method is the more you do it the better you get at it and at some point, it becomes second nature.

One thing you must remember is not to attempt to stack activities that are not conducive to the use of this method. This could cost you time in the future. Like the axiom measure twice cut once. You do not want this method to ultimately cause you to have to repeat a task and lose time in the process.

Let me give you an example, I would refrain from stacking cooking on a grill with many or any other activities, unless you have a grill that has monitors and timers. This could result in burned food, an unhappy family, and waste because the food on the grill gets ruined. The other consideration is the safety aspect of a fire, so should you really try to monitor the fire on the grill and complete other activities that take your attention away from that activity?

On the next page you will see a flow chart of the

stacking method demonstrating a possible process. Following this as a guide, pick a few activities in your compartments and create your own flowchart that you believe you could work with and accomplish using the stacking and packaging method. If it seems viable, try to put it into practice. Start slowly and work up to multiple activities that require less than complete attention to see if this strategy will work for you. Not all strategies work for everyone, do not be discouraged if this one is not for you. It is just one of a myriad of ways to conserve the time you have available. It is not a magic bullet that creates time instead it allows you to utilize the time you have to your advantage.

"The more I learn, the more I realize how little I know"

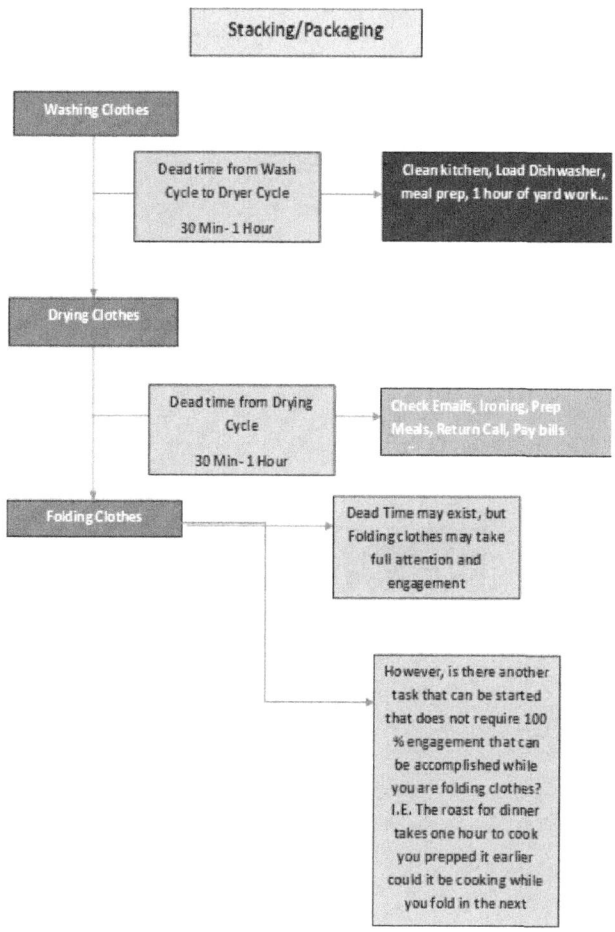

"The more I learn, the more I realize how little I know"

UNDERSTANDING AND USING TIME

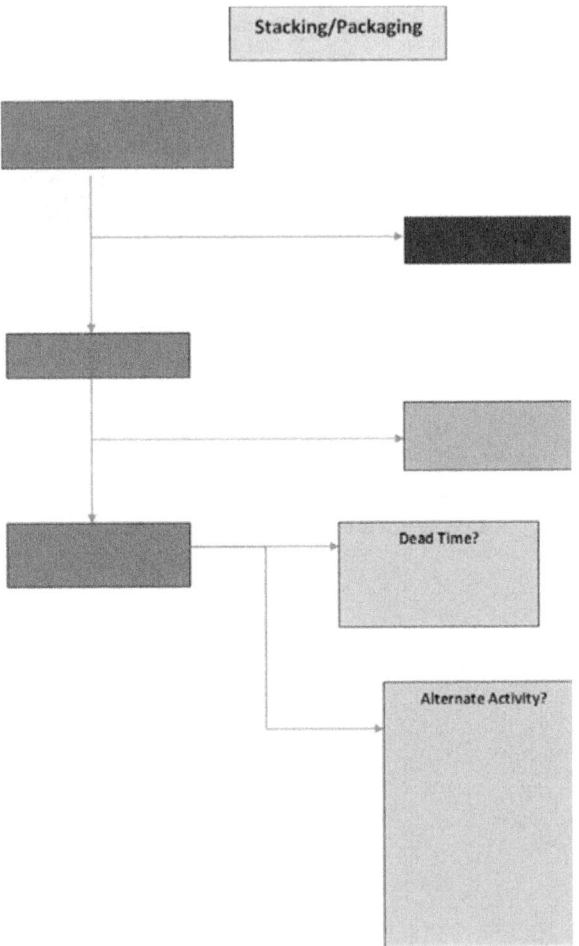

"The more I learn, the more I realize how little I know"

Chapter: 3

Time Robbers

Two of the most common issues that affect our ability to manage the limited time we seem to have available in a day are sadness/depression and procrastination.

Sadness, for most people, can be managed to a degree but no matter the level or the cause, sadness can torpedo our ability to actively engage in everyday activities and for many, causes them to make errors at work and in relationships. This may not seem like a huge deal on the surface but let us consider some jobs and make sure that my concern in this area is justified.

Let us say you are having major surgery, and your doctor is suffering from some type of sadness generated by some factor occurring recently in his/her life. What if the success rate for your procedure is 90%? These are great odds for most medical procedures that involve human actions and mechanical and electronic technology. I estimate that in general sadness, if not managed properly, can reduce focus and one's ability to perform even the most menial tasks by as much as 10% or more

"Sometimes silence Is louder than a thousand voices"

depending on the individual and level of expertise in the field. If your doctor is average now the success rate for your procedure goes from 90% to 80%. Still good odds for success, right? But also consider how many doctors work alone. Who else is involved in the procedure working at their optimum or are they at 80%; 50% due to some unknown simple factor like unhappiness or sadness? Are they even slightly distracted while programming a machine needed for your procedure, preparing the medicines or drugs to put you under?

Considering this, at any time a 90% success rate procedure due to something simple, as a few people being affected by sadness, could reduce the potential effectiveness of the surgery to 75%.

What started out as great odds can slowly dwindle to being marginal or to not being so good at all. Many would argue that the chances of several people ending up in the same room with the same concern is improbable at best. How many times have you been driving and there is almost no one else on the road but you still manage to meet with that only other person driving at a four-way stop. Scary, isn't it? Some theorists have discussed this, and I believe they reference it as the "law of attraction", introduced by William Walker Atkinson in his 1907 book "Thinking Vibration or the Law of Attraction in the Thought World".

You may have also heard of situations where two ships collide on the ocean. How does this occur? I would conjecture that when you consider these random occurrences, the chances of the six people involved in an average surgery procedure having some concern that affects their ability to perform at an optimal level increase greatly, especially when you consider the effect one individual's mood can have on another's.

More of a concern than general sadness or unhappiness is depression, especially if it is clinical and debilitating. Depression can be so psychologically incapacitating as to totally shut down a person's ability to function. This is like the action of unplugging a radio or vacuum cleaner or disconnecting your phone or computer from its battery or Wi-Fi. Anyone suffering from ongoing bouts of depression should seek proper medical intervention.

Depression and sadness, to a lesser degree, can keep

even the most focused individual from being able to manage time or the items in the compartments that take up so much space in our mind that need to be carried out.

There are some tools that many professionals will ask their clients to attempt before going to a more aggressive approach to deal with depression. In the next few pages, I will summarize a few tools I have used that have helped me to manage, not conquer, recurring bouts of depression, sadness, and unhappiness.

I call these, "Ten ways of getting over the hump." Using the ones that work for you and discarding the others.

Before we get into the details, it is important to understand the symptoms of depression according to (Mayo Clinic, John's Hopkins University). If you experience five or more of the following symptoms each day or most days over a consistent span of time you may be headed into or embedded in a major depressive mood or episode.

- Depressed or irritable mood
- Sleep problems (too much or too little not caused by vocation or medication)

- Change in interests or lack of interest in things you once cared a great deal about
- An unrealistically low self-image as compared to your peers and/or excessive guilt about something over which you have little or no control
- Extremely low general energy even after proper diet
- Extreme decline in self-care in all its facets, proper diet, exercise, personal maintenance i.e., showering/bathing, combing hair, makeup if it applies…
- Change in appetite
- Easily agitated by minor issues
- Panic attacks/ Anxiety
- Suicidal thoughts plan or actions, self-harm of any kind.

Based on the above, you have a parameter by which to judge if you might be depressed or headed into a depressed state. The question is "Now what?"

The following coping skills may help, but remember, there is no shame in seeking professional help if these strategies do not work for you according to (Harvard

Health, Mayo Clinic). In fact, you should seek help. The true shame is not asking for help when it is needed.

1) Create meaning in your life. The best way I have found to do this is to be of some service to others. This does not have to be something grandiose or big. It is seeking something even small outside yourself that helps someone else. I have never given any amount of time to help someone else that did not in some way enrich my own life and or my own experiences, helping others usually changes your mood in a positive direction.

2) Concentrate on attainable goals not the lofty ones. Create as many small successes in your life as possible. Try to make the goals SMART as well. That is Specific, Measurable, Achievable, Realistic and Time based.

3) Find your happy place by doing some of the things that bring you joy. Find things in your life to be grateful for. Journal these things and review them on a regular basis.

4) Stay focused on the present, this is called mindfulness by specialists in the field of psychology.
5) Exercise and eat right. Research has shown that even moderate exercise can improve mood. Eat food that improves mood. Lower the intake of fast and processed foods and high carb foods.
6) Find and engage with positive people who lift you up not tear you down.
7) Get enough sleep.
8) Do not take other's actions personally.
9) Find your spiritual center.
10) Try breathing exercises for relaxation.

If these methods fail, I suggest that you seek help from a specialist or professional. If they do help, you can pull yourself out of the mire and get back to using your time wisely and emptying each compartment of the tasks therein. These two main time killers now are somewhat under control, never gone, but managed.

"Sometimes silence Is louder than a thousand voices"

Chapter: 4

Procrastination

The next time killer is procrastination. Procrastination is the other constraining factor to proper use of time. Procrastination is simply the action of delaying or postponing something. This in and of itself causes inaction or the wasting of valuable time.

Most of us are guilty of procrastination from time to time, mostly since there is always something more exciting or engaging to do than work or the projects or daily tasks we should be accomplishing.

The truth is procrastination is a massive waste of the precious gift of time we have been given. It can destroy your ability to be productive at work, at home and in relationships, and even in many areas of self-improvement. Several surveys according to (Grodella.com) have shown that an individual can waste between 45-60 days each year procrastinating. This is the same as wasting between 3-4 hours a day on valueless activities. So, to reach our goal of improved not perfected time utilization, we must

"Lies are like weeds in your garden. They comeback repeatedly to haunt you, confuse you, cause you additional work and diminish your available time for other things."

develop strategies that allow us to curb the procrastination affecting our lives.

Listed below are a few suggested ways to act on procrastination, also listed are the types of procrastination that affect our lives.

The types of procrastination are called by different names but can generally fall within the following categories:

Type 1 – Perfectionist

Perfectionists pay so much attention to each detail to get things right that they often never get started or they have so many ideas that they cannot settle for one to work on. This type should concentrate on the purpose of these tasks and allot time limits to each to deal with this type of concern. Generally, this helps a perfectionist complete each task within a time frame.

Type 2 – Dreamers

Dreamers enjoy making the plan, not doing the work toward the completed project. This kind of individual should use the SMART planning framework to force themselves into action. Dreamers usually have fantastic ideas but can sometimes have great difficulty getting started. Using the Smart technique as

"Lies are like weeds in your garden. They comeback repeatedly to haunt you, confuse you, cause you additional work and diminish your available time for other things."

mentioned earlier can get them started; Specific, Measurable, Attainable Realistic/Relevant and Time-Bound goals.

Type 3 – Avoiders

Avoiders fear they are not capable of success at some tasks and therefore do not act, so, there is no chance of being criticized. Avoiders should tackle what they consider the worst first so as not to get trapped in the avoidance cycle. Break down tasks into small bite sized chunks. Consider that you must create a thousand-page report as part of a project. Do not concentrate on the 1000 pages. Concentrate on the introduction, then the contents page or agenda, then assign time to complete each section until the project/report is complete.

Type 4 – Crisis Makers

This type of individual usually waits until the last minute to get started on any project or activity. They are generally the bane of group projects, especially if they have the knowledge needed for the project's completion. They feel that when rushed to meet a deadline they perform better. If this is your type consider the technique called the Pomodoro

"Lies are like weeds in your garden. They comeback repeatedly to haunt you, confuse you, cause you additional work and diminish your available time for other things."

technique, developed by Italian entrepreneur Francesco Cirillo (https://www.pomodorotechnique.com). This method focuses on working in short, intensely focused bursts, and then giving yourself a brief period to recover and begin again.

Type 5 – The Busy Procrastinator

This type has trouble prioritizing tasks either because they have too many on their plate and they refuse to work on what they consider unworthy of their time and attention. This type must get their priorities in order. Important tasks regardless of how you feel about them must take precedence over tasks that are less important. Just because you see an email that says its urgent does not necessarily mean it is important.

How to Break the Cycle of Procrastination

- Break the work into smaller pieces.
- Ensure that your environment is conducive to completing the task(s) at hand.
- Use the SMART technique to create a detailed timeline and specific deadlines to get items completed.

"Lies are like weeds in your garden. They comeback repeatedly to haunt you, confuse you, cause you additional work and diminish your available time for other things."

- Eliminate the causes of your procrastination (Facebook browsing, YouTube, cat video watching, catching up with your favorite stars next meal i.e.).
- Change your companions to those that induce you or motivate you to action.
- Find a friend that can keep you focused and can be honest with you
- Speak your goals aloud to others. This generates a responsibility to complete the goals.
- Find someone who has already walked the path you must go, get their advice on how to continue and achieve.
- Review your goals. It does not hurt to walk away for a moment and come back to the project with a little more clarity. Sometimes you really cannot see the forest for the trees.
- Simplify, Simplify, Simplify… Do not make any project or activity any harder than it must be. One simple example of this is, having the right tool makes any job easier. If you need a

"Lies are like weeds in your garden. They comeback repeatedly to haunt you, confuse you, cause you additional work and diminish your available time for other things."

Philips head screwdriver it does not matter how many flat head screwdrivers you have.

"Lies are like weeds in your garden. They comeback repeatedly to haunt you, confuse you, cause you additional work and diminish your available time for other things."

Chapter: 5

Conquering Worry

Another possible factor affecting our proper use of time is worry or more specifically, overcoming, and/or managing worry.

When we worry about specific things in our life it can become debilitating and hinder our ability to focus on tasks at hand. The things over which we worry about can be expansive and lifelong issues or simple things we have no control over like one's height. Dale Carnegie had a list of principles that help you overcome worry. I will paraphrase these in hopes that this time-honored knowledge helps you stop worrying and get started on the tasks at hand.

Here are a few ways to begin the process:

1) Live in day long compartments. Shorten this to the items you have control over at the present time and can act on.
2) Practice facing your troubles:
   A. Ask yourself what is the worst that could happen.
   B. Prepare yourself for the worst.
   C. Think of a way to ensure the worst will not happen.

"If you are not feeling well, you may need some Son light."

3) Remember the price that worry can cause for your health and mental well-being

Analyze Worry
1) Make sure you have all the facts.
2) Weigh the facts and come to the best decision based on the facts.
3) Act based on the facts.
4) Think of it in these terms:
    a. What is the problem?
    b. What are the causes of the problem?
    c. What is the possible solution(s)?
    d. What is the best solution considering all the facts?

Ending the Worry Habit
1) Stay busy and engaged.
2) Do not let the little things become big things.
3) Do not worry about the inevitable.
4) Control your level of anxiety. Only give any issue the level of concern it is worth.
5) The past is the past, you cannot change it, so, do not worry about it.

Creating a Mental State of Peace and Wellbeing

"If you are not feeling well, you may need some Son light."

- Think positive by filling your mind with as many positive thoughts as possible.
- Try not to hold a grudge nor act on it.
- Appreciate gratitude from others, but do not expect it.
- Learn from not only your mistakes, but also the mistakes of others.
- Help others.
- Pray
- Rest
- Exercise
- Be your own cheerleader

Great Work Habits

1) Clear your desk of any items that can be solved immediately.
2) Prioritize your work in order of importance.
3) When faced with a problem, if possible, solve it immediately if you have all the facts necessary to make a logical decision.
4) Delegate things that should be delegated.
5) Manage projects not people.
6) Enjoy your work or find different work you can enjoy.

"If you are not feeling well, you may need some Son light."

Chapter: 6
ZERO TALENT

The following things require extraordinarily little from you other than your desire to do them and they can and will directly affect the impression people have of you at work, at leisure and as a part of your family. These are the things that require zero talent or intelligence but can aid in your success and proper use of time as you move through life. They may seem simple, but you would be surprised how many people fail at these simple techniques or items. Then others build their opinions based on their inability to master or achieve these skills. So, let us get into them and discuss them a little and how they affect our lives.

Be On Time - Unless you are the boss, it is critical to be on time for work. This may seem simple, but all of us know people who not only waste their time, but ours and other's time because they simply cannot be on time for a meeting to present their part of a project or some other important part of a technological project. Being on time not only tells others you value their time, but also the importance of the work. It also tells them you value your own time and that you respect yourself. There are many workplaces where

People make excuses to do the things they want to do, and they make excuses "so they won't have to do what they should do..."

failure to be on time consistently can and does result in termination from employment no matter how wonderful a worker you happen to be. The other concern about this issue is that failure to be on time usually causes a cascade effect of issues that seem to happen because of the fact you were late. The truth is, the issue may have happened anyway, but the fact that you are late intensifies the negative impact of events that are directly related to your tardiness. For example, you spilled your coffee, but, if you have plenty of time it is not a major issue, only an inconvenience. But if you are running late you rush to clean it up, and you rush out the door, but the door locks and you forget your keys. The original problem becomes exasperated by the fact that you were rushing because you were running late.

So, the simplest thing to do is to plan your day accordingly and be on time.

Make an Effort- - Sometimes what you are asked to do seems far beyond your skills or way beneath your intelligence and somewhat insulting. If you work for someone, most times you have very little control over the assignments you are given, nor the difficulty or simplicity the assignments may require. Also, the

People make excuses to do the things they want to do, and they make excuses "so they won't have to do what they should do..."

company that hires you usually does not know how smart you are or where your true experience lies related to the company's needs, so the easiest thing for them to do is start off small to lessen the potential damage. In these types of situations, you do have control of another factor and that is giving your best effort regardless of the task. This does two things for you. If it is a simple task, you have saved yourself useful time to use in other endeavors. If it is difficult and your goal is to impress, move onward and upward, then you can complete the challenging task promptly and be a candidate for the next more challenging task and make it beneficial for you and the company you work for. All the while, you are creating tools you can use, even if working for someone else is a temporary career move for you. It costs you absolutely nothing to put forth an effort that requires no extreme intelligence, just desire.

Display High Energy - This may be more difficult for some than for others but having energy and getting enough rest helps you to be alert and actively engaged in your work and during your leisure time. Having high energy allows you to accomplish more in less time and often more accurately because your

People make excuses to do the things they want to do, and they make excuses "so they won't have to do what they should do…"

attention to detail is greater when you have high energy.

Have a Positive Attitude – This is more important than any other thing you can do that will cost you nothing. Having the right attitude can take you further than you realize. People inherently want to help people who have the right attitude. They are willing to train, promote, assist, and make special arrangements for the people who bring the right attitude to work. From personal experience in HR, education, corporate, and energy fields; I have seen people go out of their way to help those who have the best attitude when at work.

Be Passionate - This means that you have intense, strong feelings or beliefs, and that you care about what you are doing. It is inherent to most individuals that if they care about what they are doing, they will do a much better job. Doing a better job enhances all other parts of your work and leisure life experiences. Also, when you do an excellent job and are passionate about your work, you save time and money not only yourself, but for the business as well.

Use Good Body Language – This has many parts, the first is to maintain a culturally appropriate appearance and

People make excuses to do the things they want to do, and they make excuses "so they won't have to do what they should do..."

have good eye contact. This does not mean having a constant unending blank stare, but it does mean that you are showing the person that is talking to you or vice versa, that you are paying attention. This also shows the other person that you are engaged in and are actively listening to and not just hearing what they are trying to share with you. Nodding your head also shows engagement, giving a firm handshake, having an upright and open posture, and leaning in (not creepily) to show engagement.

Be Coachable – This is simply being willing to learn, open to new experiences, available to become actively engaged and most importantly, listening for understanding.

Give Extra Effort – This is being diligent, industrious, buckling down and giving all you've got to whatever endeavor you have chosen. Again, this does not cost you time, it just requires putting forth the effort which ultimately saves you time. It may not feel like it while you are in the process, but it usually gives you more time in the end.

Be Prepared - It is important, even if you do not know everything you should know, that you are ready to learn and willing and eager to engage in whatever

People make excuses to do the things they want to do, and they make excuses "so they won't have to do what they should do..."

activity that is your responsibility. Never allow excuses to be your default position. "Excuses are monuments to nothing, building bridges to nowhere. (Vernon Brundage Jr.)." Therefore, if your plan is to end up nowhere then be prepared.

Have a Strong Work Ethic - It costs you nothing to be willing and ready to work. People recognize and reward a strong work ethic. The reward is sometimes less important than the recognition. Recognition can easily lead to career advancement. Nonetheless it is more important to realize that working diligently and continually at a losing cause is a vast waste of time. I suggest you always remember that each activity has its own ROI (return on investment) and if the return on investment does not enhance your life in some way by default, it is diminishing your life and robbing you of time that could possibly be better utilized. The ROI for each activity is not as easy to see as it may seem. Some people feel that idle time always has a poor ROI, but rest can increase productivity to make up for the time spent at leisure. I will discuss leisure time and exercise time later but keep in mind that both leisure and exercise time may seemingly have a poor ROI, but the reality is quite different.

People make excuses to do the things they want to do, and they make excuses "so they won't have to do what they should do..."

It is not my desire to sound preachy or to tell anyone the best way to attack their problems but to give a few tools that have allowed me to have as many as three concurrent careers moving in a positive direction at the same time. I highly suggest in all relationships, conversations and interactions, individuals should follow a simple and Biblical mantra: Specifically, the Bible councils the importance of restraint in conversation. It indicates the wisdom is depicted by people who use few words and listen more. In my life I have noticed that the more words people use, the more wrongdoing or misunderstanding turns out to be the result. In my mind this means that whether you believe in the Bible or not it is better to hold one's tongue than to speak recklessly.

People make excuses to do the things they want to do, and they make excuses "so they won't have to do what they should do..."

Chapter: 7

Exercise and Being Idle

I have mentioned before that exercise as a part of your life takes up time but the value it returns to your life is priceless. Exercise not only improves your physical fitness but in other ways it can improve your "fiscal" fitness. A healthy lifestyle that includes exercise and eating as healthily as you possibly can and, in most cases, will extend your life expectancy, reduce your need for medical intervention, and reduce your need for certain medications. The benefits of an exercise program and proper nutrition are well documented medically so I will not delve any deeper into it here. I will say, however, that the extension of your life expectancy is directly related to time management. If you can increase the time you have by extending your life expectancy it is an obvious win, especially if these additional years, days months are healthy ones. The best way to achieve this is to find an exercise that you can enjoy or learn to enjoy. Some people enjoy dancing and if you do, make dancing a part of your exercise program. Some people run, bike, go to the gym, swim, or use yoga as their exercise. Whatever you pick I have noticed, like

"If we spend our time fixing our own issues, we may not have time to worry about other people's problems."

anything else, exercise can become a habit and produce a good feeling mentally and physically. It takes time for any new program of action to become a habit, but it is well worth it if you have an interest in extending your life expectancy and reducing the need for certain medical interventions.

Next let us discuss nutrition as part of our overall fitness goal. I have heard many people say eating healthily is expensive, time consuming and mostly that they do not want to give up the foods they love. I will agree that there may be added expense to eating healthy but, on a dollar-for-dollar basis, eating fast food daily can equal or exceed the cost of preparing food at home. The preparation of food at home, if used properly, can become a positive activity for the family. There are tons of books, articles, websites, etc., that can be used to help you decide on a proper exercise and nutrition program that fits your fitness level and lifestyle. I have used WebMD as one of my go-to sites for information and I highly suggest that before starting any new exercise regime or extreme change in your nutritional intake, consult with your primary care physician. The general numbers are good, but your personal doctor can tell you which

"If we spend our time fixing our own issues, we may not have time to worry about other people's problems."

numbers apply best to fit your situation and current medical health.

Introduction: *Being Idle*

In today's fast-paced, technology-driven world, it is easier than ever to fall into a sedentary lifestyle. Whether it is sitting for hours at a desk job, commuting in a car, or spending free time watching TV or scrolling through social media; prolonged periods of inactivity are now the norm, and not only for people in the younger generations. Being idle is easy but that does not mean it is harmless. Our bodies were designed for movement, and without regular physical activity, our health and overall quality of life can suffer. Study after study has reinforced this fact. John Hopkins Medicine.org speaks of the dangers of sitting for long periods. The American Heart Association states "sedentary jobs have increased 83% since 1950." Bass Medical Group indicates sedentary lifestyles can lead to type 2 diabetes. Web MD states that sitting too much or sedentary lifestyles can impact longevity, which cause dementia to be more likely, weight gain and deep vein thrombosis is also possible. The good news is that incorporating

"If we spend our time fixing our own issues, we may not have time to worry about other people's problems."

exercise into your daily routine—even in modest amounts—can have a profound impact on your mental, physical, and emotional well-being, which directly affects your time management ability.

The purpose of this chapter is to explore the myriad benefits of exercise, not only to prevent disease and live longer but as a lifestyle investment that pays off in countless ways. Whether you are a seasoned athlete or someone who struggles to get moving, this chapter will guide you through practical strategies to make exercise a sustainable, and enjoyable part of your life.

The Physical and Mental Benefits of Exercise

- Physical Fitness: Exercise is a cornerstone of good health. When you engage in regular physical activity, your heart, muscles, and lungs grow stronger, allowing you to perform daily tasks with more ease and energy. Studies have shown that regular exercise lowers blood pressure, improves cholesterol levels, and reduces the risk of chronic conditions like heart disease, stroke, type 2 diabetes, and obesity. In fact, the American Heart

Association recommends at least 150 minutes of moderate-intensity aerobic activity each week to support good cardiovascular health.

Additionally, exercise helps with weight management by burning calories and building lean muscle mass. Weight-bearing exercises like strength training improve bone density, which is crucial for preventing osteoporosis as we age. The benefits extend to improved balance, flexibility, and posture, making injury and falls less likely.

- Mental Well-being: Physical activity is as important for mental health as it is for physical health. When you exercise, your brain releases chemicals called endorphins, which trigger positive feelings and reduce the perception of pain. This "runner's high" is often associated with intense exercise, but even moderate activities like walking can release endorphins.

Moreover, exercise is a proven tool for managing stress, anxiety, and depression. It

"If we spend our time fixing our own issues, we may not have time to worry about other people's problems."

can act as a buffer against the emotional strain of daily life, reducing the levels of stress hormones like cortisol while increasing brain function and emotional resilience. Studies show that regular exercise helps with memory, focus, and creativity.

- Aging and Longevity: Exercise is often called the fountain of youth. A study by the National Institutes of Health found that even small amounts of physical activity could extend life expectancy by several years. Activities that promote cardiovascular health, muscle strength, and flexibility not only lengthen your life but improve the quality of those extra years. Rather than struggle with immobility or chronic pain in old age, physically active individuals are more likely to be independent, mobile, and able to take part in the activities they love. Simply said, if you want more time, then exercise to increase your life expectancy. Also, it's important as indicated before that any unhealthy habits that can affect your life expectancy need to be

"If we spend our time fixing our own issues, we may not have time to worry about other people's problems."

addressed. Lifestyles and habits such as sleep deprivation, sitting too much, smoking, social isolation, ongoing stress, worrying too much, and eating an unhealthy diet also affect life expectancy.

Fiscal Fitness: Exercise as an Investment

- Lower Medical Costs: Regular exercise can save you significant amounts of money over the course of your life by reducing the need for medical interventions and medications. According to a study published in *The Lancet Global Health Journal June 26, 2024*, physically inactive people face 20–30% higher health care costs than active individuals. By maintaining good physical health, you are less likely to require treatment for lifestyle-related diseases like heart disease, hypertension, or diabetes—conditions that are expensive to manage and often lead to further complications. Reduced illness adds time for other more fun and productive uses of your time.

"If we spend our time fixing our own issues, we may not have time to worry about other people's problems."

- Increased Productivity: Exercise is not just about saving on healthcare—it also improves your productivity and time management. Research shows that physically active employees are more focused, have sharper cognitive function, and take fewer sick days than their inactive counterparts. Many companies are beginning to understand the link between exercise and productivity, offering gym memberships, fitness classes, or even yoga breaks at work. By investing time in your physical health, you are ultimately investing in your career, personal projects, and overall quality of life.

Exercise and Life Expectancy

- Maximizing Life's Time: One of the most significant benefits of exercise is its potential to increase your lifespan. A 2018 study in the *Journal of the American Medical Association* found that individuals with high fitness levels lived on average, 5 years longer than those with low fitness levels. However, the real reward is

"If we spend our time fixing our own issues, we may not have time to worry about other people's problems."

not just living longer, it is living better. Those extra years tend to be healthier, more mobile, and more fulfilling when exercise is a regular part of your routine.

- Incorporating Exercise into a Busy Schedule: Many people struggle to find time for exercise, especially with work, family, and social commitments. But the truth is, fitting in exercise does not require hours at the gym. Small adjustments like walking or biking to work, taking the stairs instead of the elevator, or doing a 10-minute workout during lunch can make a significant difference. You can also do multiple things—watch your favorite show while doing a quick workout or use your time on the phone to pace around the house. Finding those pockets of time throughout the day to move adds up over time.

- Exercise Habits: Research suggests that it takes about 21 days to form a new habit, but for exercise, it may take a little longer. The key is consistency. Start with manageable goals, such as committing to 10 minutes of

"If we spend our time fixing our own issues, we may not have time to worry about other people's problems."

exercise a day, and gradually increasing the time or intensity as it becomes a part of your routine. It's important to focus on making exercise a long-term commitment rather than a short-term goal. Over time, the habit will become second nature, and you will start to crave the physical and mental benefits that
- exercise provides.

Enjoying the Process: Finding the Right Exercise

- Exploration: Exercise does not have to be a chore—it can be an enjoyable part of your daily life. The key is finding the right type of physical activity that suits your preferences and lifestyle. For some, this might mean a high-intensity cardio workout, while for others, a calming yoga session or leisurely walk might be more enjoyable. If you are not sure where to start, try experimenting with different activities: swimming, dancing, running, cycling, strength training, or even outdoor activities like hiking or kayaking. No one knows themselves better than you do, pick an activity that resonates with you, then exercise becomes much easier and more enjoyable.

- Case Studies: Take, for example, Sarah, a 45-year-old mother of two, who never considered herself athletic. After trying different activities, she discovered a love for Zumba, a dance-based workout. What started as a fun hobby quickly became part of her routine, and she credits it with improving her mood, energy levels, and even her relationships with her kids. Similarly, Mark, a 60-year-old retiree, found that cycling allowed him to explore unfamiliar places while staying fit. By trying different activities, both Sarah and Mark turned exercise into something they looked forward to.

- Combating Boredom: One of the reasons people struggle to maintain an exercise routine is boredom. To keep things interesting, try mixing up your workouts. You might run one day, lift weights the next, and attend a dance class later in the week. Group exercises, like joining a sports league or

"If we spend our time fixing our own issues, we may not have time to worry about other people's problems."

attending a class with friends, can also make workouts more social and fun. Another tip is to set small goals for yourself—whether it's increasing your running distance, trying a new yoga pose, or lifting a heavier weight, these mini-milestones can help keep you motivated.

Nutrition: Fuel for a Fit Life

- Debunking the Myth of Cost: It is a common misconception that eating healthy is expensive, but with a little planning, it is often less expensive than eating fast food or dining out. A McDonald's combo meal can cost between $8–$10, while a healthy, home-cooked meal of chicken, brown rice, and vegetables can cost around $5 per serving. Buying in bulk, meal prepping, and avoiding processed foods can also help keep costs down.
- The Role of Food in Fitness: Your diet plays a critical role in fueling your workouts and aiding in recovery. For example, complex

carbohydrates like whole grains provide sustained energy, while protein supports muscle repair and growth. Healthy fats from sources like avocados, nuts, and olive oil are essential for brain function and hormone regulation. A balanced diet ensures you are getting the vitamins, minerals, and nutrients needed to support an active lifestyle.

- Balanced Approach: Healthy eating does not have to mean giving up your favorite foods. Instead of concentrating on restricting your diet, aim for balance in your diet. The Pereto rule (80/20 rule) often referred to as "The Pareto Principle "discovered by Vilfredo Pareto, an Italian economist in 1897; is a great approach—80% of the time, eat nutrient-dense, whole foods, and 20% of the time, allow yourself indulgences. This way, you can enjoy the occasional treat without derailing your fitness goals.

"If we spend our time fixing our own issues, we may not have time to worry about other people's problems."

Consulting a Professional

- The Importance of Individualized Plans: While general guidelines for exercise and nutrition are helpful, they do not always account for individual differences. Your age, fitness level, medical history, and personal goals all influence what type of exercise and diet is best for you. That is why it is important to consult with a healthcare professional before making any drastic changes to your routine. They can give personalized advice and help you create a plan that is both safe and effective.
- Personal Experience: For example, someone with a history of joint pain may need to avoid high-impact activities like running and instead focus on low-impact exercises like swimming or cycling. A healthcare professional can help assess your current fitness level, recommend exercises, and ensure that you are progressing safely. Please contact your primary care physician and develop a plan that suits your medical needs.

"If we spend our time fixing our own issues, we may not have time to worry about other people's problems."

Overcoming Obstacles to Fitness

- Common Excuses: Lack of time, energy, and motivation are some of the most common excuses people give for not exercising. However, these obstacles can often be overcome with a bit of planning and creativity. If time is an issue, try incorporating short, high-intensity workouts like HIIT (high-intensity interval training), which can provide significant health benefits in just 20–30 minutes. If you struggle with motivation, find a workout friend, or sign up for a class that holds you accountable.
- Getting Started: To help readers get started, here is a simple 30-day action plan:
    - Week 1: Walk for 10 minutes each day.
    - Week 2: Add a 10-minute strength-training workout twice a week.
    - Week 3: Increase walking time to 20 minutes and incorporate some light stretching.

"If we spend our time fixing our own issues, we may not have time to worry about other people's problems."

o Week 4: Introduce one new activity, such as biking or yoga, for variety.

By gradually increasing the intensity and duration, you'll build confidence and make exercise a sustainable habit.

Conclusion: The Long-Term Vision

- Consistency Over Perfection: The goal of this chapter is not to make you an elite athlete, but to encourage you to make consistent, positive changes to your lifestyle. It is not about perfection—missing a workout or indulging in a treat does not negate your progress. What matters most is sticking with it over the long term.
- Visualizing Success: Take a moment to imagine yourself a year from now, having incorporated exercise into your life. You will have more energy, feel stronger, or notice a difference in your mental clarity and emotional well-being. Fitness is about the journey, not just the destination, and every small step you take today brings you closer to

a healthier, happier future. As a side benefit you are healthier, happier, and able to use your time more efficiently during life's most fun and/or beneficial circumstances.

"If we spend our time fixing our own issues, we may not have time to worry about other people's problems."

Chapter: 8

Post Traumatic Stress Disorder and Time

The National Institute of Health stated that Post Traumatic Stress Disorder is defined as an anxiety disorder that can result from a traumatic event in one's life. This term is usually used in relation to military service, but it applies to survivors of any of life's traumas, including but not limited to, sexual abuse, sexual violence, mental abuse, mental violence, childhood traumas of all kinds and even social/emotional traumas.

Post traumatic stress can be a common reason for people to be less effective in their everyday lives. PTSD can cause individuals to struggle with various cognitive, emotional, and behavioral challenges, causing a direct impact to their daily lives. One of the areas profoundly affected by PTSD is management of time.

The effect of PTSD on cognitive functioning has been medically proven in several studies and are directly related to the individual's ability to manage time. Below are some of the ways in which PTSD can impact time management.

If you do not like the results you're getting, you may need to change the actions you're taking.

- Difficulty Concentrating – Individuals experiencing PTSD often have trouble in maintaining focus on tasks and assignments. This can lead to project delays, procrastination, and an inability to plan properly and/or complete tasks in a timely manner.
- Memory Problems – any type of trauma, especially as indicated above can affect memory thereby making it difficult to remember deadlines, steps required to complete a task, and appointments. This forgetfulness can result in missed opportunities and a sense of chaos and confusion in everyday life.
- Flashbacks and Intrusive Thoughts – People suffering with PTSD can become overwhelmed by thoughts directly related or tangentially related to the events that caused their initial trauma, and the worst part is the intrusive thoughts can come at any moment without warning. This may cause them problems such as being inattentive and mentally absent in meetings or lacking focus

If you do not like the results you're getting, you may need to change the actions you're taking.

during activities. This can be very problematic if the activity they are involved in is inherently dangerous, for example electrical work or working with dangerous machinery.

Emotional Challenges

Emotional challenges and difficulties are a part of PTSD symptoms, and they also directly affect daily functioning at work and in daily life.

- Anxiety – anxiety can easily cause individuals suffering with PTSD to feel overwhelmed by the simplest tasks. The result can be avoidance behaviors. This can and does lead to tasks being either avoided, neglected or in some cases disruptive behavior.
- Depression and Lack of Motivation – depression in most cases coexists with PTSD causing low energy and lack of motivation. Again, lack of motivation can lead to the inability to prioritize tasks and to poor time management.
- Hyper-vigilance – Some PTSD sufferers experience a constant state of being overly stimulated leading to exhaustion and reduced

If you do not like the results you're getting, you may need to change the actions you're taking.

ability to focus on tasks. This state of mind can lead to inefficiency and inability to manage time and can cause them to fail to care about consequences.

Behavioral Consequences

The behavioral aspects of PTSD also play a role in time management issues:

- Avoidance: People with PTSD may avoid situations, tasks, or people that remind them of their trauma. This avoidance can lead to procrastination and failure to complete necessary tasks on time.

- Disorganization: The failure to categorize the cognitive and emotional challenges faced by those with PTSD can lead to disorganization in daily life. Disorganization makes it difficult to create and follow a structured schedule, further complicating time management.

- Sleep Disturbances: PTSD often leads to sleep problems, including insomnia or nightmares. Poor sleep quality affects overall energy levels and cognitive functioning, making it harder to manage time effectively.

If you do not like the results you're getting, you may need to change the actions you're taking.

Strategies for Improving Time Management with PTSD

While PTSD poses significant challenges to time management, there are strategies that can help:

- Structured Routine: Establishing a daily routine can provide a sense of predictability and control, helping to manage time more effectively.

- Task Breakdown: Breaking tasks into smaller, manageable steps can reduce the feeling of being overwhelmed and make it easier to complete tasks on time.

- Mindfulness Practices: Mindfulness (paying attention, living in the moment, and accepting who you are) then, begin to concentrate on proper breathing techniques which can help you stay in the present moment and reduce the impact of intrusive thoughts, while improving focus and time management.

- Therapeutic Support: Cognitive-behavioral therapy (CBT) and other therapeutic

If you do not like the results you're getting, you may need to change the actions you're taking.

approaches can address the underlying cognitive and emotional challenges of PTSD, aiding in better time management.

- Use of Technology: Utilizing reminders, alarms, and planning apps can help compensate for memory issues and assist in keeping track of tasks and deadlines.

Conclusion

PTSD can significantly impact an individual's ability to manage time due to cognitive, emotional, and behavioral challenges. Understanding these challenges is the first step in developing effective strategies to cope with and improve time management. With the right tools and support, individuals with PTSD can regain a sense of control over their time and daily activities.

If you do not like the results you're getting, you may need to change the actions you're taking.

Chapter: 9

P Five

Introduction to P Five

In the journey of personal and professional development, managing time effectively remains a constant challenge. It's one of the few resources we all have in equal measure, yet how we choose to spend it determines our successes, our growth, and ultimately, our satisfaction. One of the primary culprits of wasted time is a lack of preparation, a lesson that we can mitigate by using a principle known as "P Five": *Proper Preparation Prevents Poor Performance.* This maxim is more than a catchphrase; it's a mindset that, when practiced diligently, can transform how we manage time, tackle projects, and deliver results in both personal and business spheres. One of the main reasons in everyday life that time is wasted is the fact that we as humans sometimes fail to prepare properly. To make sure that in my business life this is not as big a problem as it could have been, my team and I began practicing the 5 Ps. The 5 Ps are an acronym for Proper Preparation Prevents Poor Performance. This was established to make sure we were actively working toward being successful.

Voters deserve the leaders they allow to be elected.

Even when it seems that you are spending an inordinate amount of time preparing for a meeting, presentation, lecture, or project; the time spent "getting it right" cannot be overstated. This is what I mean when I say proper preparation. Proper relates directly to the task at hand. Preparation simply means what it says, having put in place the necessary parts to complete the project and correct information at the exact moment it is required.

This does not mean that in all cases things will go swimmingly but it will make the meeting, lecture, project, or presentation achieve the minimum desired impact. This is the prevention of mediocre performance part of the equation.

The other factor is the willingness to elicit the aid of anyone who can assist you in preparing properly for the specific activity that you are involved in. Whether you are a seasoned veteran or new to the work world, this is a good maxim to go by. Whether your tool is the computer, internet and AI or colleagues with tremendous amounts of knowledge or a combination of the two, this is a way to ensure you will not fail.

The Role of Proper Preparation in Time Management

Voters deserve the leaders they allow to be elected.

Preparation isn't merely about completing tasks or checking off boxes; it's about intentionally creating a pathway that allows for smooth execution of responsibilities. Whether it's preparing for a business meeting, a presentation, a complex project, or even a simple conversation, adequate preparation helps prevent last-minute scrambling, which not only wastes time but also adds stress and leaves room for error.

When we dedicate time upfront to ensure readiness, it might seem counterproductive to those who prefer diving into action immediately. But experience teaches that well-prepared individuals rarely face the same frustrations or roadblocks that tend to derail those who haven't put in the groundwork. Proper preparation acts as a form of time insurance, making it easier to execute plans without avoidable delays or unnecessary detours.

Breaking Down P Five: The Practical Components

1. **Proper Preparation**
    - In the context of P Five, "proper" means appropriate to the specific task. Proper preparation includes:

Voters deserve the leaders they allow to be elected.

- o Understanding the task's objectives and requirements.
- o Researching necessary background information.
- o Organizing materials, tools, or resources.
- o Identifying potential questions or concerns that could arise.

The preparatory phase should be customized to meet the unique needs of each task, as this ensures efficiency and makes the time spent on preparation more purposeful.

2. **Preventing Poor Performance**

    Poor performance often stems from inadequate planning and preparation. Through preparation, we reduce the likelihood of unforeseen obstacles, allowing us to focus our energy on making an impact. For example, preparing a well-structured presentation not only saves you from fumbling over words but also increases audience engagement and confidence in the

Voters deserve the leaders they allow to be elected.

message you're delivering. Even if the preparation doesn't guarantee flawless execution, it significantly mitigates the risks of mediocrity.

3. **Seeking Help and Resources**

    Preparation isn't always a solo endeavor. Sometimes, leveraging expertise—whether it's the input of a colleague, tools like computers and AI, or research from knowledgeable sources—can provide valuable insights and prevent oversights. This collaboration not only enhances the quality of preparation but also speeds up the process, ultimately making it more efficient.

Strategies for Implementing P Five in Daily Life

- **Set Aside Dedicated Preparation time**

    Building preparation time into your schedule is crucial. For instance, if you have a major presentation next Friday, start blocking out smaller segments of time early in the week to focus solely on getting your materials, research, and visuals together. This incremental approach prevents the need for

Voters deserve the leaders they allow to be elected.

an all-nighter on Thursday and allows for a more thorough, less stressful preparation process.

- **Break Down Larger Tasks**

    Break down complex projects into smaller, manageable tasks. This approach prevents being overwhelmed and encourages consistent progress. By focusing on smaller goals, you make more effective use of your time and minimize the chances of getting stuck in unproductive, last-minute rushes.

- **Identify High-Impact Tasks**

    Not all tasks require the same level of preparation. Identify which meetings, projects, or deliverables will have the greatest impact on your goals and focus your preparation efforts accordingly. This prioritization ensures that your energy and time go toward preparing for high-impact tasks while allocating less time to less critical ones.

Voters deserve the leaders they allow to be elected.

The Ripple Effect of P Five: Enhanced Efficiency and Productivity

When consistently practiced, P Five can transform how efficiently we operate in various areas of life. Proper preparation not only prevents poor performance but also leads to better decision-making, increased confidence, and the ability to handle unexpected challenges with ease. For example, let's consider two employees who are scheduled for a project presentation. Employee A spends time researching, organizing, and seeking insights from experienced colleagues. Employee B decides to "wing it," believing their knowledge of the subject will suffice. While both may succeed to a certain degree, the polished, thoughtful presentation by Employee A will likely resonate more with the audience, achieving better results and saving everyone's time in clarifications or follow-ups.

Avoiding the Trap of Over-Preparation

While preparation is essential, it's possible to over-prepare, causing diminishing returns. Avoid letting preparation become a form of procrastination. Set a specific time limit for preparation tasks and stick to it. If you find yourself continuously revising and

Voters deserve the leaders they allow to be elected.

refining without reaching a conclusion, you may be over-preparing.

The Role of Technology in P Five

Today's technology offers numerous tools to streamline preparation:

- **Project management tools** (like Trello, Asana) help you organize tasks, deadlines, and resources.

- **Collaborative platforms** (such as Slack or Microsoft Teams) allow teams to share ideas and information in real-time, streamlining preparation.

- **Artificial intelligence** can speed up research, generate outlines, and even provide predictive analytics that can help anticipate possible challenges in a project.

Leveraging these tools can make the P Five process more efficient and help prevent common pitfalls associated with poor preparation.

Conclusion: P Five as a Time-Saving Mindset

Adopting P Five as a time management strategy will enable you to accomplish more with less stress and fewer obstacles. It empowers individuals to approach

Voters deserve the leaders they allow to be elected.

tasks with a sense of confidence and readiness, improving their chances of achieving their desired outcomes. Remember, proper preparation isn't just about spending time; it's about spending time wisely. With P Five, you're investing in a smoother, more efficient process that will pay dividends in productivity, impact, and professional success.

Voters deserve the leaders they allow to be elected.

Chapter: 10

The Dreaded Meeting

One way to save a tremendous amount of time is to manage your meeting(s) in an orderly and concise fashion. Meetings, whether by Zoom or in person are a necessary evil of most businesses and sometimes in personal interactions with other groups in which you may be a member. The problem with meetings is that they are either considered unnecessary by the people who are invited, or they take longer than they should or that they have been scheduled to last. So how do you have a good productive meeting and honor people's time? First, I think we should have a list of the items that make up a good meeting. There are many thoughts on this but below is a list that I believe encompasses many of the general thoughts around what are the elements of a good meeting.

Elements of a Good Meeting

- A Clear Agenda
- Actionable next steps
- Facilitate the meeting well
- Outcomes
- Assigned roles
- A follow-up plan

"Knowing what to do and doing it are not the same thing."

- Invite Feedback
- Set Expectations
- Start on time
- A specific Goal
- Assign Action Steps
- Attendee list(s)
- Coordinate Schedules
- Pre distribution of the agenda
- Topics, Sequences, and time allotments
- Invite the right People
- Objectives

The agenda is one of the most important places to start when planning a meeting. If you are having any difficulty creating a concise, clear, and simple agenda you may be about to have an unnecessary meeting. First is the meeting's goal or purpose. Next are the topics or objectives to be discussed during the meeting and their purposes. I suggest that you allocate time to discuss each of the topics. This can be adjusted as needed but it helps to keep your meeting on track and helps to monitor the time. It may be important also to list who handles the discussion or facilitation of the discussion of the

"Knowing what to do and doing it are not the same thing."

topics listed on the agenda. Also, if feasible, distribute the agenda ahead of time. This will allow the participants to prepare properly if they must bring or provide information that will move the topics listed on the agenda forward. The next most important thing is to ensure that the right people are invited to the meeting and if important business decisions need to be made related to the meeting, ensure that the person or persons who have that decision-making authority are present or have sent a proxy with the authority to make those needed decisions. It is frequently mentioned that facilitating a meeting well is very important. This means ensuring that you have and can maintain the group's attention at the beginning, and during the meeting. This may be done by setting ground rules and by having some type of opening that draws everyone in. It may be a joke, a story or something much simpler. Once you have the agenda, invite the right people, and have a comfortable space that is conducive to the meeting parameters then you can begin the meeting in an earnest drive toward the goals listed on your agenda. Be aware that things rarely go as planned so do not expect your meeting to either. Do what you can to

"Knowing what to do and doing it are not the same thing."

keep things on track but expect topics to arise that can sidetrack your agenda. If this happens, as quickly as possible move the meeting back to its original purpose. One way to achieve this is by using a parking lot (a parking lot is a list of items that need to be resolved that come up during a meeting but are not part of the meeting at hand) for important items that come up but are not important to the issue at hand. As a side note make sure that the parking lot items are taken care of at some point before the meeting is concluded. Another important thing to remember is to have a scribe for your meeting that takes notes and documents specific assignments, projects and/or duties that arise out of the meeting. As the meeting ends, review the assignments that arise from the meeting. Review your understanding of the decisions that were made and edit as necessary. A consensus is great but not always necessary depending on the makeup of the group. But if your team is a good one, they already realize once the hierarchy has decided, then they have a responsibility as leaders to do one of two things; support the team's decision and direction, or to convince the team that direction is not advisable, and why, then convince them to move in

"Knowing what to do and doing it are not the same thing."

an alternate direction. I suggest that at a post meeting once the meeting notes have been reviewed, edited, and approved, they are sent out to the group with the assignments listed and expected completion dates either listed if known or requested from the assigned party. Lastly, monitor and adjust as necessary until all items are completed.

Can an agenda-less meeting be productive?

There are many CEO's and other business professionals, Clergy and nontraditional leaders that feel agenda less meetings are better and more productive. The fact is that even meetings that do not have a specific agenda do have a structure and in many ways that structure is the agenda. Many people who like this meeting method feel that the general brainstorming and flow of ideas can create a crucible for new product ideas and the expression of feelings, motives, ideas, and forms of expression not allowed for with a standard agenda. If the formulation of these types of ideas and brainstorming is the goal, then an agenda-less meeting is a suitable method of achieving the goal. In these cases, time saved by achieving the goal is the true goal and time management becomes a subset of the overarching

"Knowing what to do and doing it are not the same thing."

goal of moving the business forward.

"Knowing what to do and doing it are not the same thing."

Chapter: 11

The Purpose of Time Management

Why is time management important? It is not important only for the reasons you suspect or have read in many other books or articles but because it is the singular thing in your existence that impacts everything else in your life. Time management impacts each and everything that anyone has ever told you it would but there are deeper, more otherworldly ways in which your use of time impacts, affect and guide your life. I believe you may have heard said or heard in a movie or read in a book or in an internet article or post someone say that they wish they had more time, or if I only had more time, I would have… The truth is each of us is given all the time we need not a second more or a second less. It is our use of what is given that may at times be suspect and cause us to rethink how we have used what we were given or how we should have used the time we had allotted to us. Conceptually, the hurdle I just asked you to cross is a mind boggling one. Because each one of us can think of situations where people seem to be gone too soon. But are they really gone too soon if their work on this plane is

"Sometimes God has to scream when you will not listen when He whispers."

completed? Are they really gone if we remember them? I would say they are not. The simple fact that we remember a person means they live on in us. It may not be how we want it to be or what we would prefer but it is a simple fact. These are interesting thoughts, and we may decide to delve into them later, but that is for another time. Therefore, you should manage your time more wisely.

I want you to consider doing this so that you can have a richer, more meaningful, fuller, and dynamic life. The main recipient of your successful journey here is of course yourself. Others who benefit are your family, your work group, your important contacts, and your not so close contacts. When effectively used, time management allows you to be available for your friend instead of your enemy. When properly managed, time becomes a partner that follows along the path and helps you along your journey instead of being a predator that stalks you throughout your life. Many people in western culture despise aging and many of us, if we are honest with ourselves, fear it. Let us consider that people who fear aging or despise age in general, are really in a place where they have not been using the time they have been given wisely

"Sometimes God has to scream when you will not listen when He whispers."

and are in a constant state of reliving the past moments they can never relive or redo. Wishing to undo past mistakes or relive past glories fully knowing it is completely impossible, is a monumental waste of valuable time. These types of feelings eat away at many people year after year. Even when we do not realize that this, "wish cancer" is eating away at us over and over, second by second, again and again.

Once we dispose of the disease and the wish cancer that is a part of the feeling not fact that we have wasted time, we become free to live our best lives. Making the most of each second our lives have to offer, lives best lived whether 100 years or 1 day, are lives that have meaning past the fact that you just existed. Philosophically, these things are great to discuss but the practical applications are also valuable for our everyday lives. Let us get down to a more practical mindset regarding time management.

So, the purpose of time management is simply to enhance your life in as many ways as possible. If you use your time wisely then all parts of your life are improved. Your work life becomes easier and less demanding. You have more time for family

"Sometimes God has to scream when you will not listen when He whispers."

endeavors. Personal time is expanded, and it does not feel like you are failing to do other things because you are keeping some moments for yourself. It is often said that "if it is not broke, do not fix it." This may work for many things but in life I would say that growth and change are an integral part of what makes us human. If this is so then I would say sometimes it is important that we shake things up a bit and make changes that improve, enhance, or expand our thinking, knowledge, or position in society. This means that sometimes even if it isn't broken, we should look at our processes, behaviors and uses of time and make changes that enhance our lives.

If we accept the theory, then we should consider the purpose of time management as a way of expanding our thinking and understanding how best to use what in theory seems to be a finite thing but, and in our dreams, time seems to not be finite. So, break the barriers that say what cannot be done in a certain time parameter or what should be done in a time parameter and think of ways to use the existing time to best realize the goals that you have in mind. Another theory or axiom or thought that I am sure you have heard that we need to dissect and try to

"Sometimes God has to scream when you will not listen when He whispers."

better understand is the thought that "time can be wasted." I would say that time cannot sometimes be best used the way others feel it should be used or even the way others are paying us to use time. The truth is sometimes what appears to be a waste of time is really using existing time to think through a process to reach an end. Many scientists have worked on a problem ad nauseum for years to try to reach a solution, but they never quite get there. Then someone comes in and looks at the equations that they have never worked on before and can walk right up to the whiteboard or computer screen and solve the equation. This may be frustrating for the scientists who worked so hard for so long, but their work did have an impact on the outcome. No time was really wasted. When we rest, we are refueling our minds and bodies to better use the upcoming active cycle of time available to us. Now this is not to say we as humans never use time in a way that is less advantageous to our planned ends, but it does put in context the idea of wasted time.

This may be as good a time as any to tell you a little about why I feel time management is important and how I have used it to my family's advantage in my

"Sometimes God has to scream when you will not listen when He whispers."

life.

When I returned to Memphis from escaping Hampton Institute, at the time, I was unemployed, and I needed to take whatever job I could get. I say escaped Hampton because I graduated but let us just say it was not with highest honors. I took a job substituting with the Memphis City Schools and ended up at the same school as my brother, Kingsbury High and Middle school. The principal and vice principal at the school must have seen something in me that I never noticed in myself, and they requested I be made a full-time teacher. This was an interim assignment, and I had to take courses at the University of Memphis to fulfill the necessary requirements to maintain the teaching position long term. I did this and was successful at Kingsbury. I had desires that the salary would not facilitate so I ended up taking an extra job at 7-11 overnight to bridge the gap. I did this for several years. Youthful enthusiasm and strength allowed me to do this, as well as the help of my brother who was picking me up in the morning. I changed my clothes in the car on the way to work. Ultimately, I was noticed by the mathematics advisor and was moved to Northside High School.

"Sometimes God has to scream when you will not listen when He whispers."

At the same time, I met a manager from FedEx who came inside the 7-11 every morning. He said I should consider applying to work there because of all the opportunities that the company offered. I did and was now working at FedEx as a handler and a teacher at Northside High School. Again, I was blessed with success at both jobs and got great employment reviews as a teacher and was able to help many students. While a handler at FedEx, I was told that I should apply for a training specialist position because of my teaching experience. I applied for more than 100 jobs before I was selected as a training instructor but who's counting? This was a pivotal moment in my career because I was selected for a position as a training specialist in New Jersey. I had to decide, and I chose to resign from my teaching position and take the job with FedEx. Add to this the fact that I was married, and we had a child. This was difficult but not as tough as it could have been because at that time FedEx allowed jump seating back and forth. Additionally, the salary was equal to both salaries at the time. The brief period that I worked in New Jersey was the longest period that I worked at one job. It lasted only about 18 months, and I transferred

"Sometimes God has to scream when you will not listen when He whispers."

back to Memphis and ended up being promoted to Training Manager at FedEx and teaching at Northside High School at the same time. At one point in my life, I have worked as many as three jobs successively. This does not necessarily seem within the realm of possibility but there are many witnesses from my various careers that can attest to this fact.

The highest point I reached in my work life with FedEx was Training Manager, but the most directly impactful was when I was moved to Senior Human Resources Advisor during one of FedEx's several downsizing and "employment correcting "efforts. I feel that this position was more impactful because it allowed me to help people at all levels of the organization. When I was teaching at Memphis City Schools, I had the opportunity to interact and work with a man named Jim Davis. He was Director of Labor Relations and Benefits. He noticed me, and I was promoted to his area and became a Labor Relations Specialist. Under his tutelage and after years of study, I became an asset in an area that I was not even remotely experienced. This was just a start to my blessings at MCS. I was later promoted to Coordinator of Labor Relations when Jim Davis

"Sometimes God has to scream when you will not listen when He whispers."

passed away and the Administrations changed. After this, another administration (Superintendent) was hired, and I became Director of Human Resources for the Memphis City Schools and ultimately Assistant Superintendent of Human Resources during the last administration that I worked for. Keep in mind I also was still working with FedEx in Human Resources. Both were full-time jobs, but the blessing and curse of exempt level jobs is that you are paid to complete a task and not necessarily by the hour. This can be if the person you report to allows it and gives you flexibility. It can also mean at times you feel you are working additional hours for no pay. I was blessed to be able to manage these jobs well and always received good to great reviews.

The Associate Superintendent job made me want to consider being a Superintendent and I knew the only way to even be considered was to have my doctorate; so, I started work on my doctorate three years before I left MCS. The administrations changed again toward the end of the degree program, and I ended up leaving MCS for a job with Memphis Light Gas and Water, the city's utility company. I was selected as the Vice President of Human Resources and held

"Sometimes God has to scream when you will not listen when He whispers."

that job approximately 10 years while I was still working with FedEx.

"Sometimes God has to scream when you will not listen when He whispers."

Chapter: 12

The Mindset of Time Management

The ability and desire to effectively manage the time each of us is given requires the proper approach. This attitude is generated by a desire to take advantage by utilizing each moment of our existence for a necessary end. Notice that I did not say a work end or a fun end or even a religious end. I indicated a necessary end. I used this term because each hour of each day of our lives requires a different necessity, and your mindset must be toward using the available time to that end. Humans are interesting creatures; they will expend vast amounts of energy on what they consider fun and there is truly nothing wrong with fun or using your time to enjoy yourself. In all actuality some people's lives are so set either by birth, luck, good money management or accident that they can use all their available time on leisure activities we mostly consider fun. This part of the population, when you consider the whole, is exceedingly small. The rest of us have or have opted to raise a family, work, and earn our way through society. The mindset for the latter is the one on which we will concentrate. It requires us to use the compartmentalization

"Regarding talents, attributes, and abilities....Everyone gets something, but no one gets everything

strategies I mentioned earlier in Chapter 1 once we have decided that using time wisely is important and beneficial to a healthy and happy life. The time management mindset requires the ability to see the options and choose the best use of your time. This may seem simplistic but for many people this is harder than it seems. Let us go through a few scenarios and see if our decision making is as solid as we want it to be. You have a project that is due at work, and you need to stay at work two additional hours to complete the project. This may be a career deciding project. You also in the next hour are supposed to attend your daughter's cello recital. Additionally, you have missed the last two and have promised your significant other as well as your daughter that you would be there. What is the most important use for the next two hours of your time? For most of us this is not a complicated equation. The most important option in this scenario is your daughter's recital hands down. This is not to say that the project is not important but with the limits time seem to place on our existence, I feel, and I always will, that keeping your vow to your daughter is much more valuable than the work issue. The reality is that,

"Regarding talents, attributes, and abilities....Everyone gets something, but no one gets everything

in general, there are usually other options that we either do not see, refuse to see or are blind to for myriad reasons. Take the scenario I gave you. There is always the option of requesting additional time to complete the project. Based on the way the scenario was worded it is quite possible that it was the end of the workday, and the information was not needed until the next day. If this were the case, you may lose some sleep but after the recital you could go back and complete the project and have it ready for the next morning. If you explained to your boss, the situation may have given you additional time beyond your expectations. The fact is, there are a vast number of possibilities related to any issues and the key to time management is to pick the best option related directly to the situation that exists.

The purpose of time management is to better use the most precious gift that we have, and that is time. This will mean something different to each person, but we all need to recognize its value and use it to our advantage and to the advantage of others in our community both small and wide.

"Regarding talents, attributes, and abilities....Everyone gets something, but no one gets everything

Chapter: 13

Motivation and Time Management

What motivates us to act, create, plan, execute, succeed, and believe? Is there a correlation between motivation and time management or should there be? I would say there are some baseline motivations that all humans have. These are the need to be safe, physiological, self-actualization, esteem, achievement, external incentives, love and belonging. As we review this, I believe it would be helpful to define and explain each of these motives.

Physiological Needs.

Basic physiological needs—such as food, water, sleep, and procreation—are universally essential and non-negotiable. Without these, other pursuits become irrelevant because the body cannot function optimally. For example, a lack of adequate sleep or nutrition can directly impact cognitive functions, dampening motivation and productivity. Some might replace traditional pursuits of family and procreation with personal passions or devotions, investing this need for legacy into careers, arts, or humanitarian efforts. Our commitment to meeting these needs forms the foundation for more complex ambitions.

There are some who may feel that procreation is a

less important or nonexistent need. I feel that people usually replace this need with another need or devotion to replace it.

Self-Actualization.

Self-actualization represents our drive to achieve our fullest potential, often considered the pinnacle of personal development. It's unique because it encompasses both internal satisfaction and external achievements, such as setting and reaching personal or professional goals. Yet, the concept of "true potential" is elusive—can we ever truly know if we've reached it? Self-actualization is deeply personal; for some, it's tied to career achievements, for others, its artistic expression, and for many, it lies in altruism. This need to become the best version of ourselves reflects a life-long journey, and time management becomes critical here as it ensures that we continually make space to pursue meaningful goals aligned with our values. Reaching one's full potential is a goal that many humans strive for. I wonder at times how many people truly ever achieve this. They may feel successful or not but has any of us ever reached our true potential? Can the runner winning the gold medal run faster? Would the businessperson who has become the richest person on earth truly have reached their full potential if, to that person being the most famous artist, would make them feel self-actualized? It seems so individual. But for the sake of this discussion let us keep it as simple as reaching one's potential that makes them feel content most of the time and happy at least some of the time.

Esteem.

Esteem is related to the human need to feel respected and valued by others as well as oneself. I have heard a lot of people indicate they do not care what people think but I have rarely believed this statement. We care and act on this feeling. Achievement, external incentives, internal incentives, love and belonging all come together in the choices we make. It's not just about external validation; it's also about feeling competent, confident, and valuable. This motivation often manifests through career success, recognition, or personal mastery of a skill. Although some claim indifference to other's opinions, the need for esteem is subtly ingrained in human behavior. Esteem also influences social dynamics; when we feel valued, our capacity to contribute meaningfully and support others increases, fostering community and interpersonal growth. Managing time to build self-esteem might involve dedicating time to skill

"Sweep around your own front door."

development, community engagement, or self-reflection.

To expand on this, let's delve into each core motivation, examining how these elements drive our actions and shape our sense of purpose. Exploring the relationship between motivation and time management offers insight into how we prioritize these needs and goals in our daily lives. Time management, when guided by a clear understanding of what motivates us, becomes a tool that helps us align our actions with our most deeply held desires and values.

Safety

Humans have a basic need to feel safe. Even humans who desire to compete or play extreme sports and activities generally make sure that even though the activities that they engage in are extreme, they make sure that in the context of the activity it is as safe as possible. On the lighter side we all want a safe home, neighborhood, city, and country to live in. On a grander scale we all would prefer a safer, cleaner world.

Safety is a foundational motivation, rooted in our instinct for survival. It encompasses both physical and emotional security. We naturally avoid risks that threaten our well-being, yet paradoxically, many are drawn to calculated risks, such as extreme sports, to experience growth within a controlled environment. This need manifests in our day-to-day desire for secure homes, stable relationships, and predictable routines. On a global scale, our collective motivation for a safer, cleaner world fuels activism and policies aimed at reducing environmental harm and promoting social justice. Without a baseline of safety, higher-level motivations become harder to achieve, as individuals in unsafe environments are often forced to focus exclusively on survival.

Achievement

Achievement encompasses the human drive to reach specific, often measurable goals. This can include completing a degree, running a marathon, or publishing a book. Unlike self-actualization, which is deeply personal, achievement is often more publicly recognized and celebrated. Both external and internal incentives drive this need: awards, promotions, or even a sense of personal fulfillment from reaching a target can keep us motivated. Achievement is also closely tied to time management, as it often requires structured steps, consistency, and long-term commitment. Setting aside regular time blocks to

"Sweep around your own front door."

work towards goals can ensure steady progress and reduce the risk of burnout.

External and Internal Incentives

Incentives, both external (money, awards, public recognition) and internal (personal satisfaction, pride), are powerful motivators. These incentives vary greatly among individuals; what drives one person may have little impact on another. While external incentives often serve as initial motivators, it's internal incentives that tend to provide lasting motivation, especially in tasks that require perseverance and creativity. Understanding which type of incentive drives us can help us structure our time and environment in a way that sustains our motivation.

Love and Belonging

The need for love and belonging is deeply rooted in human connection. Relationships with family, friends, and partners provide emotional support and a sense of belonging, which helps us navigate life's challenges. This need extends to feeling part of a community or a cause, contributing to a sense of purpose. Investing time in relationships and community-building efforts foster stronger bonds, which can, in turn, boost our motivation to tackle

"Sweep around your own front door."

other areas of life. The pursuit of connection often shapes our values, priorities, and even our professional paths.

Motivation and Time Management: A Symbiotic Relationship

Motivation and time management are inherently linked. Motivation helps prioritize tasks and fuels the energy needed to accomplish goals, while effective time management provides the structure to channel that motivation productively. Without time management, even the most motivated individual can feel overwhelmed. Conversely, a strong time management strategy without intrinsic motivation can lead to burnout or apathy. By aligning our schedules with our motivations, we create a life of purpose, balance, and steady progress.

In sum, understanding our baseline motivations and linking them with our approach to time can significantly enhance our ability to achieve, connect, and ultimately, to self-actualize. This interplay between motivation and time management is a powerful tool in shaping a fulfilling, well-rounded life.

"Sweep around your own front door."

Chapter: 14

Time Management Methodology

One example of the proper use of time and using a methodology, in actuality, to preserve time and improve your performance and hopefully your life is understanding and using a test taking methodology. One good example of this that I have used and have shared with others who have used it and have been successful, is by means of multiple-choice tests. Many of the tests a person will take throughout life are either multiple choice or true or false. The methodology I am about to espouse I cannot claim ownership of or tell you from whom I learned the skill, but I know it works. The first key to taking any test is making the decision to be prepared to pass the test. This requires something many of us dislike but is a part of the equation and that is study and repetition. There is no effective way to enter a testing environment without proper preparation. After that, the skills for success come in and they will save you time and emotional distress. Once the study is complete you must understand that for most multiple-choice tests there are generally four or five

Listening to others Is very different from hearing what they say. We spend a great deal of time while listening, preparing to respond; not to hear and understand

possible answers to the question that is posed. In most, if not all cases, two of these answers are completely and totally without merit and can easily be discarded as not possible as the correct answer. This gives you a 40%-50% chance of getting the correct answer, 50% in the case of a four-response test and 40% in the case of a 5-response test. If you have really studied and prepared for the test and there are 100 questions even if you are the worst test taker in history, you should be able to answer 50% of the questions without a problem because you know the answers. With a fifty percent chance on the answers you do not know, even by guessing, you should get half of the remainder correct. This means that just by guessing you should get 25 of the remaining 50 questions correct. At this point you have a score of 75% on the test. For many applications and environments that is enough to pass. You can improve this number or lower it by the level of preparation you are willing to prepare for on the front end. A well-prepared person who has studied the material will usually be able to get the correct answer out of the remaining two answers no less than two

Listening to others Is very different from hearing what they say. We spend a great deal of time while listening, preparing to respond; not to hear and understand

thirds of the time even if they have test anxiety. Doing math again, you know 50 % of the answers because you studied. You are well prepared so you can use educated guessing to get 75% of the remainder correct, 75% of the 50 remaining questions gives you a score of 87.5 which is well above passing on most tests. Now we will go to the other considerations related to multiple choice tests. Along with the fact that two of the answers are obviously wrong. Most test makers generally make one of the answers perfectly correct and the remainder close to correct but not the best answer. Therefore, proper preparation is important. It makes sure you can tell the difference between the best correct answer and the one that is close to correct. The time you save in preparing for a test ensures you will not waste your valuable time having to take the test again. There are situations that I am aware of at some jobs that have "one and done" tests. This means you may not get a second chance right away to pass the test. This may mean losing out on a job opportunity in the process.

I generally tell people to answer the questions they

Listening to others Is very different from hearing what they say. We spend a great deal of time while listening, preparing to respond; not to hear and understand

are sure of first. This seems counter intuitive to some, and you must be incredibly careful to make sure that you answer the question correctly as you go through the process. The next step is to go back and work on the ones you think you have the best chance of getting corrected based on the fact you have studied and know for a fact that two or three of the remaining answers are wrong. Continue the process until it is completed and check your work but be careful of second guessing yourself. Rarely have I changed an answer once I finished a test, exam or other assessment, to what I thought would be a better or more correct choice and changed it to a different answer. I will only do this if I know for sure that I am making a correct change. This can happen because in many tests the answer to some questions may lie in a future question or by reading further, you may spark a memory that ensures you know an answer.

Having a similar process works in many other areas as well. Process and procedure for many people is a norm. If flying by the seat of your pants is more your style it is not the end of the world. Use processes and procedures in the areas of your life that in some way,

Listening to others Is very different from hearing what they say. We spend a great deal of time while listening, preparing to respond; not to hear and understand

shape, form or fashion, need them and use your natural inclination when it is more conducive to what you are doing. I feel it is good for everyone to get out of their box and try something new and different. Whether it is a new way of doing things or trying a new hobby, sport, or other activity to add spice and excitement to your life. Being a great user of your time includes most importantly enjoying all aspects of your life, which is the essence of what millions of self-help books are referencing when they talk about work life balance.

The most important aspect of motivation is action. It is important that you do not let inaction cause you to waste time. In general, this is called procrastination. There are many excuses not to take an action, but very few are justified. If something is important enough to take up space in your brain as a needed action, then you must plan to get started immediately. As you have heard many times before, excuses are monuments to nothingness. If you allow yourself to make them, then your expectation should be to achieve nothing. The result of inaction is wasting time. The most precious commodity we have and as

Listening to others Is very different from hearing what they say. We spend a great deal of time while listening, preparing to respond; not to hear and understand

I have indicated before, the one we do not know how much or how little we have is time so let us not waste a moment of it. Fill your mind with words of action. I will, I can, I am able, and ultimately your mind and body will be in sync and action will be your normal process.

Let me take you down a path I have already been down. For most of my youth I was overweight with all the associated problems and concerns of every fat kid that happened to me over the years. Only the fact that I had a few teachers who encouraged me and managed my education lessened the pain and caused me to have some growth and sense of worth amongst my peers. At some point at the end of high school and planning for college, there were things I wanted for myself and losing weight was one of those things. I am not sure if it was the pressure of my peers, the pain of the rejection from many school mates of the constant bullying that caused my desire to lose weight.

When deciding to invest your time in a project, educational endeavor, activity, or long-term issue remember to consider the ROIV- return on

Listening to others Is very different from hearing what they say. We spend a great deal of time while listening, preparing to respond; not to hear and understand

investment value. Many projects are necessary, and the time invested versus the outcome have a level of equity that makes them practical and there is a level of common sense in completing the project. Then there are assignments related to either work or school that may require an extended use of time and effort. For most work-related projects, the ROIV is somewhat obvious. Your employer has in a straightforward way purchased your time for some defined period, then they have assigned you an activity to complete commonly known as your work. The ROIV for these tasks is usually your paycheck for hours worked. For those of us who work in hourly functions there is also the consideration of possible extended hours or overtime where the needed work extends beyond the initial time purchased from the worker. This is generally called overtime and the ration for this time is generally paid at a higher rate than is normally paid. It may be time and a half, double time, or in some circumstances even triple time. In these cases, the employee needs to make a conscious decision as to whether the ROIV is worth the extended work hours, provided the

Listening to others Is very different from hearing what they say. We spend a great deal of time while listening, preparing to respond; not to hear and understand

employee MOU- Memorandum of Understanding or Union Contract of employment provides the ability to accept or deny the extended work periods. Let us say in this case that the option belongs to the employee. In these cases, the person must decide if the return on investment is high enough to justify the additional expenditure of time. If the employee will lose time better spent with family, getting appropriate rest, or engaging in another activity or fulfilling another promise, one has made the acceptance of the additional time and one half or triple time. The factors that need to be considered in the equation seem simple at first glance but if we look at them, they become more complicated than we would otherwise assume. Albeit the money derived from the overtime may in many ways seem to enhance the individual's financial position. This increased financial position is worth the reduced amount of time spent assisting your children with their homework, playing with them, spending time with your significant other, resting or providing service to others in all forms. This turns a small math problem into trigonometry or calculus. The reason this is true

Listening to others Is very different from hearing what they say. We spend a great deal of time while listening, preparing to respond; not to hear and understand

is because of simple cause and effect principles. Every decision we make impacts on others that interact with others in many ways both seen and unseen both in the present and potentially in the future. Because of this truism, each time impacted decision should be weighed and measured not only carefully but insightfully regarding as many factors as one feels are important. From a family perspective, missing your daughter's recital may be okay viewed from one perspective but wholly unacceptable from another. The uniqueness is bound up in the fact that your daughter will never be that age again and never perform this act again. It is inherent that in humans even though we may give the same performance repeatedly, usually every performance is unique. Then there is the impact on your daughter's emotional maturity or lack thereof. Well, she thinks Dad or Mom must work so I understand, or Dad and Mom chose to work, and I am not particularly important to them. Also involved in this is the reaction of your significant other and their impact on your referencing the decision you opt to make. I want to try to make a judgement call for you on this one but as you can

Listening to others Is very different from hearing what they say. We spend a great deal of time while listening, preparing to respond; not to hear and understand

guess, if there are multiple children the impact of these types of decisions on how you allocate your available time may snowball. The decision matrix for an exempt employee is remarkably similar without the additional renumeration paid by the employer. Exempt employees do not get additional pay for additional hours worked as a rule. There are circumstances where an employer can pay additional pay to exempt employees as per their individual policies. The other side of this coin is that even though it is expected that exempt employees will work a normal 40-hour work week, there is much more flexibility at some corporations. Some weeks they may work 40, 50 or 60 hours a week and other weeks they may work 30 or 20 if the expected work is completed. These differences may minimize some of the concerns raised regarding non-exempt or hourly positions. FLSA states that an exempt employee must be paid a salary above a certain level and work in administrative, professional, executive, computer related or outside sales roles. Generally, exempt employees are paid a set salary annually. FLSA does not mandate an exempt employee to

Listening to others Is very different from hearing what they say. We spend a great deal of time while listening, preparing to respond; not to hear and understand

work a 40-hour workweek. However, many employers have policies or procedures that require exempt employees to work 40 hours a week or be subject to disciplinary action up to and including termination. The obvious question that comes to mind is does an exempt employee have to work 40 hours a week. The answer is that it is based on the company's policies but also whether an exempt employee works 30 hours or 60 hours their pay does not fluctuate unless there is another company policy that allows for additional compensation.

Listening to others Is very different from hearing what they say. We spend a great deal of time while listening, preparing to respond; not to hear and understand

Chapter: 15

Sharing your time with Others

I have never noticed that any time spent helping others has been an improper or poor use of the limited amount of time we have on this planet. In general, I have witnessed that it not only enhances the life of the person being helped, but, in an even greater sense, it enriches the life of the person helping others. In my opinion, it is very similar to planting a seed and waiting for it to grow. Most gardeners know that preparing the soil and planting the seed is only the beginning. The nurturing, watering, and tending of the garden is just as important as the decision to plant a seed. If you properly do all the steps, then usually a beautiful garden is the result. It is interesting to me that in each moment of our lives we are planting a seed either for ourselves or others. Additionally, it amazes me that people sometimes have no idea what type of seed they are planting. Each interaction we have with others plants a seed, not only in the other person but in ourselves as well. Also, the seeds that we sow are in many ways the result of the seeds others have planted in us. There are many people that will say a good tree will only produce good fruit and

"How do you earn people's trust? Do you believe that the people you lead trust you? If not, what will you do about It?"

a bad tree will only produce bad fruit. I will admit in general this feeling may have some validity. But with people, I have noticed that to a varying degree, people we feel may not be the best people can have offspring that are generally good and vice versa. Take a moment and think of the people you know and see if your personal experience validates or dispels this hypothesis.

Unlike seeds in nature, a truly good outcome can come from what appears to be bad seeds. In my mind, this is caused by the interactions along the way that enhance, change, grow, invigorate, enable and inspire the individual with a poor start in life to change and become all they can be and more. So, spend time giving and helping, growing, passing on knowledge, lessons learned, lessons not only from your successes but your failures as well. Do not limit your sharing with family and friends but with anyone willing to listen to counsel. This type of time usage will bear fruit now and into the future.

The Cost of Allowing Others to Take Your Time

It is hard to hear but for some of our time, as I have said earlier, we have decided to trade for money and have called it a career. Whether it is a job in the

"How do you earn people's trust? Do you believe that the people you lead trust you? If not, what will you do about It?"

traditional sense or an entrepreneurial pursuit, some of us allow others to take some of our precious time thinking we owe it to them. If not, it's not because of how it would look if we did not do it, but for religious or other personal reasons. As I have indicated earlier, I think the joy of helping others is a wonderful use of our time. However, I do not want you to get caught up in thinking you owe the best of your time to others. I have heard of many situations where a person has spent their lives in ways that cause their current and later years to be less enviable and children, if there are any, are tasked with several options regarding dealing with loved ones.

If the money is available, they use it to take care of aging parents. This has a time cost but it's relatively inconsequential in the grand scheme of things. You set it up, you make sure the bills are paid, make the cursory visits, and move on with your life. Sounds a little crass when you simplify it down to the facts doesn't it? But it is what it is. Next there is the situation where money is an issue, or no money exists to help with the situation.

In an event where little money is available the decision must be made to use your and your family's

"How do you earn people's trust? Do you believe that the people you lead trust you? If not, what will you do about It?"

personal time to care for the ailing relative. This expenditure of time can come at a cost of days, months, years, decades, or scores. The result of this loving decision to bring a relative or other person into your home or care for them in their home as long as possible comes at a cost of not only time, but emotional stress on your family and friends, the depletion of resources not to mention the physical implications and loss of time to enjoy life as you move through time.

So what point is made by these realizations? Most importantly, it is for you to remember that you are the manager of your time, and you must manage how much of your time is reasonable to share with others. This is a fluid issue, and it changes depending on the specific factors that affect your situation. I am not in any way saying not to help others. I am saying you are just as important as anyone else in your life. Self-care, as it is called now, is particularly important and self-care begins by understanding that your time is valuable, it is a limited resource and since we have no idea how much we have, we should cherish every minute. Share and assist yes, but not to your own detriment. This naturally leads us into a self-care

"How do you earn people's trust? Do you believe that the people you lead trust you? If not, what will you do about It?"

space and why self-care is so important. There are too many psychologists and psychiatrists to count, but one thing they agree on is the value of self-care and not allowing others to infringe on your need and time to engage in self-care activities. So, let us discuss for a moment why self-care has value.

Self-care provides for the individual a way to maintain and enhance their overall wellbeing, balance life's obstacles and successes and in many ways create joy. Let us review some of the reasons self-care and saving time for self is so important.

Physical Health – Self-care activities including exercise, proper nutrition and getting enough sleep have the side benefit of helping you maintain physical health throughout your life, increases and supports immune system health and can reduce the risk and onset of some chronic diseases and illnesses.

Mental Health – Meditation, nature walks/runs and/or journaling can reduce stress, depression and anxiety caused by daily activities and events. The results of these activities can and often do, provide mental clarity, a positive mindset and emotional stability.

Emotional Well-being – Self-care can and will, if

"How do you earn people's trust? Do you believe that the people you lead trust you? If not, what will you do about It?"

practiced consistently; assist you in processing emotions, dealing with one's feelings in a more productive manner and developing resilience against life's constant challenges.

Increased Productivity – When people are well rested and mentally balanced and aware of their emotional state, they tend to be able to focus better and thereby be more productive in any activity they engage.

Improved Relationships – Being self-aware and engaged in self-care causes individuals to be more centered, content, and confident leading to better engagement with others and creating more meaningful deeper longer lasting relationships.

Prevention of Burnout – Valuing self-care can ensure that as life comes at you, you can withstand the potential burn-out that can occur from maintaining day to day activities that deplete you of the emotional ability and resources to cope.

Self – Awareness – Self-care forces you to tend to your own needs, set limits and become aware of your desires and how they fit into a balanced life. Self-awareness allows you to define your life's goals and aspirations within the defined parameters of your life.

Empowerment – By prioritizing your needs through

"How do you earn people's trust? Do you believe that the people you lead trust you? If not, what will you do about It?"

proper use of self-care techniques, your own wellbeing becomes as important as everyone else's and fosters a sense of growth and autonomy, confidence, and a growth in self-esteem.

To summarize, essentially self-care is vital for leading a balanced healthy lifestyle. It enhances your life in all the ways that allow you to use the time available to you more wisely and enjoy more fulfillment in any activity you choose to engage in.

"How do you earn people's trust? Do you believe that the people you lead trust you? If not, what will you do about It?"

Chapter: 16

How Utilizing Proper Listening Techniques Can Impact Your Use of Time

Have you ever noticed that when you are talking to another person, a friend, a child, a co-worker, a business associate or a relative that somehow the message you intend for them to receive is somehow quite different from the message they received? In my mind, this is because humans have an unfortunate tendency not to be able to consistently listen to what is being said. For some reason they immediately start thinking about their response prior to hearing and listening to the message being relayed to them. This is why everyone should practice listening techniques that not only aid in general communication but reduce the number of misunderstandings between people and most importantly, save you time. Many novels, essays, and Op Ed's talk about this as active listening. It is more about "being present" and listening not to respond but to understand and showing interest and engagement in the conversation and information being shared. There are many side benefits to listening well. First, of all, it is a core leadership skill. It promotes reduced anxiety and

"Just because a problem isn't dealt with; it doesn't cease to be a problem.?"

depression, enhances the building of positive relationships and allows you to experience empathy. So, how do you develop and improve this skill? After listening and allowing the other person to complete their thoughts, ask thoughtful, engaging questions. I generally would say in these types of situations, "what I heard you say was…." and If I get it right, then I have shown engagement. If not, the other person could correct me, and we can move the conversation along.

The main time saving in this is, there is no confusion about what was said and usually no need to have that specific conversation again. It may lead to better relationships that enhance both parties' lives. I have always seen an enhanced life to not only to save time, but time in which both are equally important. Imagine your life if for every conversation you had, the other person understood you. You never had to repeat yourself because of a misunderstanding, you never had to apologize because someone heard something other than what you meant. I know for me that I would have probably saved five years of my life in meaningless repetition of conversations, apologies and/or fights that would not have occurred if either

"Just because a problem isn't dealt with; it doesn't cease to be a problem.?"

I or the other party had listened for understanding with empathy and caring.

"Just because a problem isn't dealt with; it doesn't cease to be a problem.?"

Chapter: 17

Managing How You Interact with Others

Many people confuse hearing a person or conversation with listening to a person during a conversation or oration. The reason this occurs in my opinion is that the mind tends to wander because of all the thoughts that are unresolved. Also, daydreaming can cause us to lose focus on the here and now.

I have found that when I am truly listening to a person, I can easily restate back to them what they have said. I have noticed that when I do this, it really makes the person happy to know that they have been heard and understood. The conversation usually goes something like this, "I listened to what you said but I want to make sure I heard you correctly. I heard you say…." The response is generally something like, "Yes you got it." Or that's not what I said or meant at all." If the latter is the case, then you must ask them to repeat, because you may have missed something they said. Continue the process until you have a good, if not perfect, understanding of what the issues, concerns, or ideas are.

"Working hard to create something no one wants is a definition of insanity. Creating something everyone needs that they did not know they wanted, is genius."

You must be incredibly careful not to purposefully misinterpret what a person is trying to convey to you. Some leaders, managers and supervisors do this purposefully as a tactic to achieve an edge in the conversation, meeting, or discussion. They feel this throws the other person off their game or disrupts their thinking process.

If you think about it, all of us hate to be misunderstood, misquoted, or lied on. If you want to severely damage a personal, professional, or incidental relationship, do either of these things on a regular basis, and I can guarantee you will be successful at undermining the communication process.

You may ask why I indicate that you should be slow to speak. I say this because words are powerful and much more importantly, they can be very hurtful to yourself and others. I suggest you calmly and calculatedly go over what you want to say in your mind; (your personal supercomputer) the myriad effect that your next words may have on the other person. By doing this on more than one occasion, I have avoided problems and conflicts between family,

"Working hard to create something no one wants is a definition of insanity. Creating something everyone needs that they did not know they wanted, is genius."

co-workers, colleagues, and incidental contact people.

Road rage does not just happen. There is usually a trigger. You may not be the main cause of the difficulty that a person is having, but you may be a person who is attacked because you have become the final straw that sets that person off. When you hurt others the ability to work together is eroded the same way trust in a relationship is eroded when the trust between them is reduced by lies and deceit. These become needless barriers to success in relationships, projects, and daily activities. Remember, as the Bible says, "a soft word turns away wrath." It is possible to give the worst news to a person, in the proper way and not escalate an already tense situation. In my past careers, I have had the unfortunate responsibility of terminating an employee. Being kind and considerate during these times is vitally important. I tried to be as respectful, clear, concise, and informative as possible during these situations. If allowed, I covered in general how we arrived at this point, answered all questions that I legally could, and attempted to allow the person to leave with the maximum amount of

"Working hard to create something no one wants is a definition of insanity. Creating something everyone needs that they did not know they wanted, is genius."

dignity possible. Nine times out of ten, if employees have been managed properly, they are aware that their performance or behavior was/or has not been acceptable. The proper amount of corrective action along the way has been attempted before arriving at the point of ending the relationship. Yes, it is a relationship like many others. To some, you need to remember they are not just losing a job, but a family as well. When handled well these types of situations end decently. When handled poorly you can end up as in the movie 'Falling Down' starring Kirk Douglass, or in a Postal event like we have read about too many times in the past.

Being slow to anger is an easy decision in most situations. It is understandable that in some situations anger is necessary and unavoidable, however, being slow to anger is more about having all the facts so that if you must be upset, your anger is first, directed properly; second, motivated; but with a just cause, and third, it fits the situation you happen to be in. It would be unreasonable to be so angry about a dropped egg on the kitchen floor that it caused you to have an aneurism or hurt a loved one; but if you

"Working hard to create something no one wants is a definition of insanity. Creating something everyone needs that they did not know they wanted, is genius."

found out there was an unfortunate situation involving your child and an adult, extreme and directed anger may be unavoidable. Some may disagree but I would say it would be justified. Just ask yourself this question; in the grand scheme of things is the issue I'm about to blow up about and damage my relationships, really that important? In most general business situations, it isn't. On the personal side, a lot of times the anger issue may be justified. If they are not, take a breath or ten, if necessary, and think about the best way to move forward. Remember, many times when people attack you, it is not about you. It is really something going on with them or in their life that is generating angst and fueling the potential conflict.

The end of everyone's rope looks a little different. This requires a level of sensitivity to the feelings of others that we may not realize. Many of us have heard the saying "God does not put more on us than we can bear", but what each of us can bear is unique and quite different. The differences can be because of one's upbringing, current circumstances, education, or the lack thereof, race, gender, sexual orientation,

"Working hard to create something no one wants is a definition of insanity. Creating something everyone needs that they did not know they wanted, is genius."

and/or a myriad of other factors. The point is, we tend to view other people's problems from our vantage point using our perspectives, morals, feelings, history, and upbringing. This is not a fair way to judge how any event may be affecting or impacting another person. Developing the level of empathy necessary to go outside of yourself and feel from another person's perspective may seem difficult at first. However, if you try to understand more about your friend, lover, colleague, or co-worker prior to an outrageous event occurring, you have a basis for a higher level of empathy and understanding.

Having this knowledge may in some way help you understand how others compartmentalize their concerns that can ultimately become a compartment in your group of concerns. With our goal being the best use of time, perfecting this skill obviously yields our base goal of saving us time both for ourselves and others.

So how does this relate to proper time management? If you spend very little time being angry or having to figure out what others have said, you have automatically improved your usage of time and have

"Working hard to create something no one wants is a definition of insanity. Creating something everyone needs that they did not know they wanted, is genius."

ensured that the time you have is not spent managing your anger or apologizing for things that were said or involved in doomed relationships, friendships or work relationships.

> "Working hard to create something no one wants is a definition of insanity. Creating something everyone needs that they did not know they wanted, is genius."

Chapter: 18

Generational Differences and Their Effect on Your Usage of Time

The generational differences between each age group are the causes of communication and other problems between parents and their children, some companies and their workers, and some individuals and others whom they encounter. More specifically, from a more personal perspective as a baby boomer, and after discussions with my wife, who is on the cusp of being a baby boomer, we had a level of respect for our parents that kept us from doing and saying some things to them that we felt were disrespectful. This was ingrained in us to the point that even if they were wrong, we held back and tried to find alternative ways to get our points across to them, even in situations where we knew we were right. This was sometimes even to our own and/or their detriment.

Millennials, based on our current interactions and those of our friends, co-workers and family, suggest, if not proves, that the millennial generation does not have a level of respect for their parents. Additionally, they are for the most part consumed with a level of selfishness or self-absorption that does not allow

"The grass always looks greener on the other side of the fence, but when you go over there it is the same color as yours.".''

them to consider other people's feelings. This is exposed in family, work, personal and other relationships that we have seen. Now the responsibility of how each generation reacts to the next or the past generation is, in fact, the result of the actions of the generation that raised them.

Millennials were raised in an era that created participation awards and the devaluation of being the best by accepting that participation awards are a way of supporting failure or that a lack of trying is okay. This is in essence de-emphasizing the notion of reaching for success or greatness.

However, being exceptional has continued. Olympic records still fall. Gymnasts still reach new heights of success. This supplicates the question of whether a perfect "10" is all there is. So, we must ask ourselves, is this generation that we have created, who seems so selfish; the ones who have made many of the advances that we have today? Many people question whether or not the Instagram, Facebook, and Tic Tok generation are better for us as individuals, so I think it's worth discussing. Are we as human beings connected to one another, or aren't we?

If we are more connected or less connected with each

"The grass always looks greener on the other side of the fence, but when you go over there it is the same color as yours."."

other because of the advances in technology, then, in what ways does this have an impact on the use of our time? To some it means we spend less time in personal interaction, but on the other hand, we spend an inordinate amount of time engaged with each other using the several types of social media available to us. In many ways the current technological advances will enhance our ability to use available time effectively. I am still concerned, however, that personal interaction is becoming the victim of technology. It does not feel as if we are as sensitive to the needs of others and in a way, less sensitive to our personal needs as well.

I am also concerned that the use of social media and AI can become a distraction that is not positive in the work environment and life in general. As an example, I have recently noticed that even though most cellular devices allow hands free operation, I often see drivers using their cell phones while attempting to drive. Many would say the jury is still out on whether the human mind is truly capable of multi-tasking. For years, people considered this a skill they had when they went through the interview process. New research suggests that what was once perceived as

"The grass always looks greener on the other side of the fence, but when you go over there it is the same color as yours."."

multitasking is literally not giving full attention to either of the tasks you are engaged in. If the latter is true, then driving and using your cell phone becomes the most dangerous of propositions, in the case of work, or even leisure activities, this could become very problematic. An accountant could make a one-digit numerical error that results in a massive financial liability in the books. A person engaged in a leisure activity and attempting to reach for the phone may miss an incoming concern, miss an emergency alert, or place themselves in an even more dangerous situation. From all the possible iterations of what could happen, I would err on the side of caution and try, as best as possible, to concentrate on finishing one project before moving on to another. Or, if multiple projects must be worked on in concert, do everything the available data and information allows for one prior to moving on to another project in succession. Use available downtime to research and glean the needed information that impacts each project and continue the process until completion.

"The grass always looks greener on the other side of the fence, but when you go over there it is the same color as yours."."

Chapter: 19

Rest and Wasting Time There is No Correlation…

Rest is not a waste of time, so do not feel bad about it. It might stand to reason that since I spend a good part of this book discussing time and the proper use of it that I might consider resting less than a proper use of time. Just the opposite is true. Proper rest is paramount to proper use of time. Rest enhances exercise, mental acuity, work performance and in many ways, extends life. The rest period allows not only one's mind to catch up on its necessary base line or sanity, but it is important to understand the benefit of sleep and rest. Unlike a computer or AI, or an electronic device, the brain and mind are biological computers that are used to store information, decipher and help us manage and survive our surroundings, understand complex structures, and moral and ethical concepts and apply them appropriately. The physical body needs rest and relaxation so that when it is called on to perform, it can. Associated with this is a proper diet, which we will discuss later in this chapter. As we age, our ability to repair these mental cells lessens over time, however, when we continue to exercise and rest, our body, mind and spirit can continue to function properly and efficiently for an extended length of time.

The complicated part of the rest equation is that each person is so unique and individual, that what is the perfect amount of rest, sleep, and rejuvenation for one person, is vastly different for another person.

The Power of Rest in Effective Time Management

Rest as a Critical Component of Productivity

In a society that values productivity and the efficient use of time, rest is often overlooked and often sidelined as something that stands in the way of achievement. Yet rest is not only necessary; it is foundational to achieving true efficiency and maintaining long-term health and wellness. Far from being a time waster, rest is an investment in the proper use of our energy and focus, which directly correlates to achieving our goals and performing at our peak. In this chapter, we will delve into why rest is essential, how it enhances various aspects of life, and how we can manage our time to incorporate adequate rest for optimal performance.

The Biological Need for Rest

While it might seem appealing to push through fatigue or cut back on sleep to get more done, the human body is designed with built-in limitations that should not be ignored. Unlike a computer that can run on a power source until it malfunctions, the human brain requires regular rest to recharge and function optimally. Every day, our minds process vast amounts of information, manage emotional responses, and make countless decisions and activities that consume substantial cognitive resources. Sleep and rest serve as natural resets, and replenishing these resources repairs neural pathways, making us sharper, more resilient, and better prepared for the tasks ahead.

Rest is especially crucial for our cognitive functions. The brain consolidates memories and organizes information during sleep, facilitating clearer thinking, better decision-making, and enhanced creativity. Without sufficient rest, we experience declines in mental acuity, impairing our ability to problem-solve and stay focused. Thus, if productivity is the goal, rest is not a distraction but a powerful tool to help us achieve it.

"Excuses are monuments to nothingness, building bridges to nowhere."

Physical Rest: Repair and Recovery

Physical activity and exertion, while beneficial, take a toll on the body's muscles, joints, and energy stores. Just as the brain needs rest to process and retain information, the body requires rest to recover and repair itself. During rest, muscle fibers damaged during exercise rebuilds and strengthen, making us physically more capable. This is why athletes and fitness enthusiasts prioritize recovery time—it allows for continuous improvement without risk of burnout or injury.

When we rest, our body replenishes glycogen levels (the stored energy in muscles), and various hormones involved in growth and repair, such as human growth hormone (HGH), are released. If rest is neglected, muscles cannot adequately repair, leading to fatigue, soreness, and eventually to a decrease in physical performance. The same principles apply to anyone seeking physical well-being, regardless of their fitness level.

Mental Rest: Enhancing Focus and Emotional Well-being

Just as our bodies need a break from physical exertion, our minds require intervals of mental rest to sustain concentration and emotional health. Prolonged mental strain without breaks can lead to symptoms of burnout, characterized by chronic stress, reduced motivation, and emotional exhaustion. This highlights a paradox: while working harder might seem like the path to success, it often leads to diminishing returns. Regular mental breaks, however, allow us to maintain a high level of productivity over time.

The benefits of mental rest extend beyond productivity. Regular downtime helps regulate mood and emotional resilience, enabling us to handle life's challenges with greater composure. Mental rest can take many forms—short naps, meditation, engaging in a relaxing hobby, or simply allowing oneself time to be idle. The goal is to step away from stressors and allow the mind to rejuvenate, improving both performance and quality of life.

Sleep: The Foundation of Rest

While many forms of rest are beneficial, sleep is essential. Sleep allows for a more profound level of physiological and psychological recovery than other forms of rest can provide. During sleep, the body performs maintenance tasks, repairing cells, balancing hormones, and reinforcing neural connections. Deep sleep cycles, which occur early in the night, are particularly vital for physical restoration, while later cycles help with memory consolidation and mental clarity.

Interestingly, the amount of sleep required varies significantly among individuals due to genetic, lifestyle, and environmental factors. This was discussed earlier in the text. For some, six hours of sleep may be sufficient, while others need closer to eight or nine hours. Understanding your unique sleep needs and prioritizing high-quality sleep can have a profound impact on your overall well-being, resilience, and productivity.

The Role of Nutrition in Rest and Recovery

While this chapter focuses on rest, it is worth noting that nutrition plays a significant role in how effectively our body and mind can recover. A well-balanced diet supports energy levels, hormonal balance, and cellular repair, making our rest periods more effective. Specific nutrients, such as protein, antioxidants, and omega-3 fatty acids, support muscle recovery and brain health. Hydration is equally important, as dehydration can impair cognitive and physical performance, reducing the benefits of rest. To maximize the benefits of both rest and nutrition, aim to eat a balanced diet that includes a variety of nutrient-dense foods, staying mindful of any foods that disrupt sleep, such as caffeine or high-sugar snacks consumed close to bedtime. A body well-fueled is a body well-rested.

Balancing Rest with Time Management

It may seem counterintuitive, but strategic rest is a time-management strategy. While a packed schedule might feel productive, the best productivity often comes from working smarter, not harder. Incorporating regular rest breaks throughout the day, allowing time for sleep, and scheduling non-negotiable downtime enables us to perform at our best when we are working or pursuing our goals.

Here are a few tips for managing time to incorporate rest effectively:

1. **Prioritize Sleep**: Set a consistent bedtime and wake-up schedule. Treat sleep like any other essential activity, blocking off adequate time for rest each night.

2. **Plan for Breaks**: Include short breaks in your daily schedule, particularly during

periods of intense focus. This could mean taking a five-minute break every hour or a longer break every two hours, depending on what works best for you.

3. **Use Rest as a Reward**: Completing a big project or a challenging workout is a reason to reward yourself with downtime. Use rest to celebrate accomplishments and reinforce a healthy work-rest cycle.

4. **Avoid "False Rest"**: Passive activities like scrolling through social media may feel relaxing, but they often leave us feeling mentally drained. Instead, opt for restful activities that genuinely replenish your energy, such as spending time outdoors, meditating, or reading.

Embracing Rest as Part of a Balanced Life

Ultimately, the goal of time management is not merely to do more but to do what matters with a sense of balance and satisfaction. By valuing rest as an essential part of productivity and self-care, we give ourselves the capacity to achieve our goals without sacrificing health or well-being. Rest should be

"Excuses are monuments to nothingness, building bridges to nowhere."

viewed as a source of strength rather than a lapse in discipline.

In embracing rest, we allow our minds and bodies the time to rebuild and come back stronger, sharper, and more resilient. Let this chapter serve as a reminder that effective time management is not about filling every moment with activity; it's about using each moment wisely including those moments we dedicate to rest.

"Excuses are monuments to nothingness, building bridges to nowhere."

Chapter: 20

Forgiveness and Time Management

Forgiveness is a marathon not a sprint. People hurt each other all the time, in personal relationships, in business relationships, in marriages, in friendships and in teams. The level and complexity of the hurt and pain caused by others is usually directly in line with the feelings involved between the two individuals, the level of trust that exists between them and the emotional state of the people involved. It is human nature to want to retaliate for a wrong that we feel is done to us; but like what you might see on the football field, the retaliator is usually the one who gets the flag. For those of us that are not familiar with football, a "flag" is a penalty for wrongdoing on the field of play. Sports fans hate it when this happens. There is not much you can do about it except dislike it. If you think about it, this probably happened to you in school. Another kid does something to you, and the teacher does not see it. You react in kind or worse, but you get the punishment then you say, "but he/she started it…." The point here is forgiveness. I suggest we try our best to make forgiveness a part of how we live our lives. I did not say forgetfulness, but

"It's important to ask for what you need, but more important to need what you ask for."

it is important in our ability to move on with our lives that we are able to release the hate and negativity of our past and move forward. One way to do that is to forgive those who have hurt us. The second key to this is to understand that forgiveness is a marathon not a sprint. It takes time and intention to forgive those who have hurt us. It also takes time, and it helps if the person that hurts us asks for forgiveness, but it is not necessary. It just shortens the healing process if a person recognizes they hurt you and are willing to apologize for it and ask for your forgiveness. If they do not or are not willing to ask for forgiveness the road to forgiving them is arduous and long but forgiving them is still possible. It is also the best thing you can do for your mental well-being. Harboring grudges or hating another person does absolutely nothing to that person. But it pollutes and poisons your mind and soul. It controls parts of your mind and your time that could be used for more meaningful pursuits. So, how do you forgive another person for hurting you? It is a process. The process of deciding to no longer harbor the ill feelings. This does not mean the hurt will go away immediately, but it does mean that you have released portions of your

"It's important to ask for what you need, but more important to need what you ask for."

brain to concentrate on other things that allow you to recover your time and realize that the stress and time you spent on these feelings could have been better utilized in other more meaningful endeavors for you and your family. So, even forgiveness both for yourself and others is another time saving/enhancing mechanism you can add to your arsenal of abilities that grant you a better more meaningful life. So, is forgiveness related to time management? I would say in many ways it is. First, time spent concentrating on the hurt we have incurred and moreover how we will get our revenge is not the healthiest use of our time. It also damages the mind, body and spirit. It can cause emotional trauma and an inability to focus. I understand that some traumas and events that happen in our lives are extremely difficult or in some cases impossible to get over. But even in these cases we must find ways to not allow the crushing negativity of hate and lack of forgiveness to unsettle and/or rerail or lives. We must process emotions and feelings so that we are in control and not the past events of our lives. The best way to do this is to confront the pain when we are strong enough to face them and work through a process of recognition,

"It's important to ask for what you need, but more important to need what you ask for."

action, and acceptance until we reach a level of peace which allows us to continue our lives.

Forgiveness is a significant part of personal growth, and it requires time to reflect, to heal, and to move forward. By investing time in forgiveness, you are allowing yourself to let go of past grievances and reclaim the mental and emotional energy those issues have taken from you. In terms of time management, this is crucial because unresolved emotions can be a significant drain on your focus and productivity. By forgiving, you are freeing up time and energy to pursue your goals without the weight of emotional baggage.

Remember why you want this person in your life.

If the person is still in your life who hurts you, remind yourself why you want, need, or must have this person in your life and what the protocols will be for future interactions. If it is a personal relationship and you have decided that you want this person in your life no matter what your reasons you must contend with your decision and choose

"It's important to ask for what you need, but more important to need what you ask for."

the parameters for the future of the relationship. If you truly decide to forgive the person as I have stated earlier, it does not mean forgetting the offense but using the offense. Using the offense as a basis for the future of the relationship is not appropriate and will not be manageable going forward. Forgive, set the parameters, and move forward. This will cause a breakdown in the relationship somewhere in the future. Forgive, set the parameters move forward.

If it is a situation where you must have the person in your life because it is a work or business relationship, understand those parameters as well, and move forward. The same applies to friendships and whether they should continue. This is an important step in how you move forward in any relationship. Set the boundaries by which you plan to allow the relationship to continue; and recognize that your mental health is just as important as anyone else's.

This is very important in your work relationships as well. Difficult conversations may arise, but they are

"It's important to ask for what you need, but more important to need what you ask for."

necessary and may even improve relationships.

Getting mad, feeling hurt and grieving and their effects on time management

If someone hurts you, it is ok to get mad about it. It is also okay to feel hurt. Embrace these emotions but do not let them overtake you to the point that you become frozen in time. Then grieve. The grieving process is different for everyone. Some people take a few minutes or hours, for others it can take years, and still grieve the pain that was inflicted on them. The point is that grief is so debilitating that it controls your life. Do you really want to give another person that much power over your life and the time you have left to enjoy your life? Do not let others try to control your grieving process but do understand that they would not be trying to help you if they did not care and love and want to protect you. They are not the enemy and do not treat them as such. If you are trying to help someone else, know when to walk away. Do not push too far or too much. Show your care, offer your assistance but do not pressure. You can

"It's important to ask for what you need, but more important to need what you ask for."

never fully understand the pain of others even if the same events have occurred in your life. You can only understand how the event affects you, not how it affects others. So how are grieving, getting mad, etc. related to time management? Any process we go through, especially those previously mentioned above, grieving, getting angry, etc., can take a toll on how you manage your life and thereby how you manage the time you have available. It can take some of us years to get over hurt feelings, grieving the death of a loved one or hurts caused especially by those who love us. The sad fact is that some of us never get over these things. They sit like cancer in our brains, sometimes in remission and sometimes triggered by life events; then they grow and tend to take over our lives. The thing to remember is no matter how difficult the situation, you are in control. Do not let past feelings, hurts and grief control you to the point that you lose the ability to act. Many of us want to demand that others respond like we want them to and to apologize for what they did to us. Sometimes they do, sometimes they do not. But, for those of us who

"It's important to ask for what you need, but more important to need what you ask for."

believe in God, we even have the audacity to want to second guess what has happened. The reality for those who believe, is that by allowing free will, God has allowed us to chart a path towards Him or away from Him and thus we must accept the world and the way things occur as we move along our path. Those of us who have no belief in a higher power, accept that life just happens and ultimately end up in a similar place, dealing with the events that life throws at them.

Ask yourself whether your anger is constructive or destructive.

Ask yourself this difficult question. Is the anger that I am feeling constructive to my life and my family; or is it destructive to my life and family? Is the cost of it being destructive worth it? Am I willing to let this past event destroy my present and potentially my hope for the future? Destructive anger is not only mentally problematic, but it can also cause physical problems. The anger you feel can cause you to fail at current relationships, fail your children, disregard your friends, and not apply appropriate

"It's important to ask for what you need, but more important to need what you ask for."

concentration and attention to your work. It may even rob you of the spiritual centeredness necessary to feel self-love/self-care, thereby eroding your ability to care for others. Another factor to consider is that our decision-making ability is severely compromised when one has had extreme feelings of anger. Decisions we would never make normally become realized and simple to make. This type of anger-fueled decision can damage and, in the worst cases, destroy your present and possibly your future. Consider the news stories that you have heard and seen, where a person has said that someone they never thought would do something has done the unthinkable or worse. Everyone is shocked and in total disbelief, but that is the power of unbridled anger. In some cases, the result is the ultimate time destroyer, death. In other cases, a life headed for beauty could end with a life sentence in jail. A child destined for a life we have no idea how wonderful could end in a meaningless passing caused by rage. Beautiful and promising relationships have often succumbed to the discontinuity of anger and

"It's important to ask for what you need, but more important to need what you ask for."

rage, and all these negative emotions are time leeches and time ticks that reduce the possible length and beauty a life could experience. As easily as rage and anger can fuel a negative outcome, there are instances where anger can be used constructively. For example, a teen realizes they failed a test because they refused to study; then realizes that they could have made a perfect score had they studied. So, the anger at themselves fuels the need and desire to study harder and score better the next time by using time properly and to their advantage for future success. Consider the athlete that lost a race by a few seconds and used anger or disappointment to make them try harder and the next race they won the gold. These are business and personal examples I am sure dear reader you could call to mind, where anger was used both destructively and constructively. So, consider which outcome causes you to be the best, and use your time so that you will have a better life.

"It's important to ask for what you need, but more important to need what you ask for."

Don't worry, you are not saying the offense was OK.

Forgiving someone is not saying that what they did to you was okay. What you are saying is that regardless of the offense, I choose to be okay. I am not allowing others to have enough control over my life or my emotions, that they get to decide how I feel in the present moment. What was done to me was not okay, but I am bigger and better than at that moment in time. I forgive so that I can move forward.

"It's important to ask for what you need, but more important to need what you ask for."

Chapter: 21

Practice Stress-Reduction Techniques.

Stress is a part of everyone's life so we all must find ways to deal with it. There are as many ways to deal with stress as there are ways to be stressed. Each person must look for what works for them. Meditation works for some, while exercise works for others, some people paint, some listen to music or create it. No one knows you better than you know yourself so find out what relaxes you, and practice using the technique that best helps you to lower your blood pressure and reduce your stress level.

Practice Stress-Reduction Techniques

Stress is an unavoidable part of life, whether it is triggered by work, relationships, health issues, or even minor daily annoyances. Everyone experiences stress in different ways. While some stress can be motivating (like pushing you to meet a deadline or excel at a task), chronic stress can take a serious toll on both your mental and physical health. It can contribute to problems such as high blood pressure, anxiety, depression, and a weakened immune system.

"If we all give more that we take, we will all have more than we need."

That's why it's essential to find effective ways to manage and reduce stress in your life.

Understanding Your Stress Response

Before diving into stress-reduction techniques, it is important to understand how stress manifests for you personally. Stress affects everyone differently, but it typically triggers a "fight or flight" response in the body. This response causes a surge of stress hormones (like cortisol and adrenaline) that prepare your body to deal with immediate danger. While this response is helpful in short bursts, chronic stress keeps the body in a constant state of alert, which can lead to exhaustion and a variety of health issues.

Some people might feel stress in their bodies through headaches, muscle tension, or digestive issues, while others experience more emotional or mental symptoms like irritability, difficulty concentrating, or feeling overwhelmed. Recognizing how stress shows up in your life is the first step in finding techniques that work best for you.

"If we all give more that we take, we will all have more than we need."

Exploring Stress-Reduction Techniques

There are countless ways to manage stress, and what works for one person may not work for another. The key is finding the right technique that helps you feel calm, centered, and in control. Below are some of the most common and effective stress-reduction techniques:

1. Mindfulness and Meditation: Mindfulness involves being fully present in the moment, paying attention to your thoughts, feelings, and sensations without judgment. Meditation is a form of mindfulness that has been practiced for thousands of years and is widely recognized as one of the most effective stress-reduction techniques. Research has shown that even just a few minutes of meditation a day can significantly lower stress levels, reduce anxiety, and improve overall well-being.

   There are many types of meditation, such as focused breathing, guided meditation, and body scan meditation. So, you can experiment with different methods to find what resonates with you. Apps like Headspace or Calm offer guided meditations that are easy to follow, even for beginners. Start with just five to ten minutes a day and gradually increase as you feel more comfortable.

2. Exercise and Physical Activity: Exercise is a fantastic way to combat stress, as it helps release endorphins, which are natural mood elevators. Physical activity not only improves your physical fitness but also has a direct impact on reducing stress and anxiety. Whether you prefer running, walking, cycling, swimming, or practicing yoga, any form of exercise that gets your body moving can be an effective stress-reliever.

In addition to aerobic exercises, activities like yoga and tai chi combine physical movement with mindfulness, making them especially effective for reducing tension and promoting relaxation. Stretching, deep breathing, and rhythmic movements help calm the mind and ease the physical symptoms of stress, such as muscle tightness and fatigue.

3. Creative Outlets: Creativity can be an incredibly effective stress-reduction tool. Engaging in activities like painting, drawing, writing, or playing a musical instrument allows you to express your emotions in a healthy, constructive way. These activities help shift your focus away from stressors and immerse you in something that brings you joy or relaxation.

    You do not need to be an artist to benefit from creative outlets. Journaling, for example, can be a wonderful way to process stressful thoughts and gain clarity. Writing down your feelings helps you release pent-up emotions, and over time, you may notice patterns that can help you better understand your stress triggers.

4. Listening to or Creating Music: Music has the power to soothe the soul. Whether you are playing an instrument, singing, or simply

listening to your favorite songs, music can quickly alter your mood and reduce stress. Research has shown that listening to calming music can lower blood pressure, slow your heart rate, and decrease levels of cortisol.

Creating music, on the other hand, can be an active way to relieve stress. Whether you are strumming a guitar or singing along to your favorite tunes, musical expression can channel negative energy into a positive outlet.

5. Spending Time in Nature: Nature has a calming effect on the mind and body. Spending time outdoors, whether it is walking in a park, hiking in the mountains, or simply sitting by the ocean, can help reduce stress levels. Studies have shown that being in nature lowers cortisol levels, improves mood, and enhances mental clarity. Even if you live in an urban environment, finding green spaces or taking short breaks to step outside can provide a much-needed mental reset.

6. Deep Breathing Exercises: Breathing techniques are one of the simplest and most

effective ways to reduce stress. When you are stressed, your breathing becomes shallow and rapid, which can make you feel even more anxious. By practicing deep, controlled breathing, you can signal to your nervous system that it is time to relax.

Try this simple breathing exercise: Inhale deeply through your nose for a count of four, hold your breath for four seconds, and then exhale slowly through your mouth for a count of four. Repeat this cycle several times until you feel your body start to relax. This technique can be done anywhere, making it a great tool to use in moments of acute stress.

7. Progressive Muscle Relaxation (PMR): PMR is a technique that involves tensing and then relaxing each muscle group in the body, starting from your toes and working your way up to your head. This method helps you become more aware of where you hold tension in your body and teaches you how to release it. PMR is often used as part of stress management and can be particularly effective

"If we all give more that we take, we will all have more than we need."

before bed, helping you unwind and fall asleep more easily.

8. Social Connection: Talking to someone you trust about your stress can provide immediate relief. Whether it is a friend, family member, or therapist, sharing your worries can help you gain perspective and feel supported. Sometimes, just knowing that someone is there to listen to you can make all the difference.

Additionally, spending time with loved ones or engaging in social activities can be a terrific way to distract yourself from stress and recharge your emotional energy. Social connections provide a sense of belonging and comfort, which can buffer the negative effects of stress.

Finding What Works for You

Not all stress-reduction techniques will work for everyone, and that is okay. The key is to experiment and find what resonates with you. Start by asking yourself what typically makes you feel calm or joyful, this could be anything from gardening to dancing to cooking. Once you name your stress-relief preferences, make them a regular part of your routine. Stress reduction is most effective when practiced consistently, rather than waiting for stress to build up to unmanageable levels.

Consider keeping a journal to track which activities help you the most. Over time, you will notice patterns and be able to refine your approach to stress management.

The Health Benefits of Stress Reduction

Regularly practicing stress-reduction techniques has profound benefits for your overall health. By lowering stress levels, you can improve your cardiovascular health, boost your immune system, and even improve cognitive function. Studies have shown that reducing stress also helps lower blood pressure, reduces the risk of heart disease, and improves sleep quality. Mentally, you will experience better mood stability, increased resilience, and a greater sense of emotional well-being.

"If we all give more that we take, we will all have more than we need."

Stress is an inevitable part of life, but how you handle it can make all the difference. By prioritizing stress-reduction techniques that work for you, it will not only improve your quality of life but also protect your long-term health.

Stress and Mental Health: Higher rates of stress, anxiety, or depression due to stigma, discrimination, and being a minority can impact time management. Coping with mental health challenges might affect productivity, leisure, or time spent on self-care. This is how mental health, and stress can impact your use of time and certain groups are more adversely impacted in these areas than others.

"If we all give more that we take, we will all have more than we need."

Chapter: 22

Setting Boundaries

Set Boundaries for a Healthier Life

Setting boundaries is one of the most essential, yet often overlooked, aspects of supporting healthy relationships—whether personal, professional, or even with yourself. Boundaries are the invisible lines that define how we expect others to treat us and how we interact with the world around us. They are critical for safeguarding our mental, emotional, and physical well-being. Without clear boundaries, we risk feeling overburdened, disrespected, or taken advantage of, which can lead to resentment, burnout, and emotional distress.

In this chapter, we will explore why setting boundaries in relationships is so crucial, how to effectively establish them, and how doing so can lead to healthier, more fulfilling relationships in all areas of life.

"Avoid power point blindness, where you can't see that the speaker is talking about you."

What Are Boundaries?

Boundaries are personal guidelines, rules, or limits that we create to define acceptable behavior in our relationships. They help protect our emotional, mental, and physical space, ensuring that others treat us with respect and that we treat ourselves with kindness. Boundaries are essential in every type of relationship, whether with family, friends, romantic partners, coworkers, or even in our relationship with ourselves.

There are several types of boundaries, including the following:

- Physical boundaries: Defining personal space and physical contact.
- Emotional boundaries: Protecting your emotional well-being and ensuring that others do not manipulate or control your feelings.
- Time boundaries: Ensuring that your time is respected and that you are not overcommitting yourself.

"Avoid power point blindness, where you can't see that the speaker is talking about you."

- Intellectual boundaries: Respecting differing opinions and beliefs.
- Work boundaries: Setting limits on your professional responsibilities and ensuring work-life balance.

While the specifics of boundaries may vary from person to person, what remains universal is the importance of clearly defining and communicating them to others.

Why Boundaries Are Essential for Mental Health

One of the primary reasons boundaries are so vital is because they directly affect your mental health. When you do not set boundaries, you may find yourself saying "yes" to things you do not want to do, tolerating disrespectful behavior, or feeling overwhelmed by responsibilities. Over time, this can lead to stress, anxiety, and even depression.

Conversely, when you set clear, firm boundaries, you take control of your life and protect your emotional well-being. Boundaries help you prioritize your needs, avoid burnout, and create a sense of balance

"Avoid power point blindness, where you can't see that the speaker is talking about you."

in your relationships. They allow you to say "no" when necessary and to ensure that you are treated with the same respect that you offer to others.

Key Benefits of Setting Boundaries:

- Reduced Stress: Setting limits helps reduce feelings of overwhelm by preventing others from overstepping.
- Improved Self-Esteem: Setting up boundaries reinforces your self-worth and helps you feel more confident.
- Greater Emotional Stability: Boundaries protect your emotional energy, preventing emotional exhaustion.
- Healthier Relationships: Relationships become more respectful and balanced when both parties know and respect each other's limits.

Setting Boundaries in Personal Relationships

In personal relationships, such as those with friends, family, or romantic partners, boundaries help support a sense of individuality and respect. It is important to

"Avoid power point blindness, where you can't see that the speaker is talking about you."

communicate your needs clearly and assertively, whether it is about how much time you spend together, what behaviors are acceptable, or how you handle conflict.

For example, in a romantic relationship, you might set boundaries around your need for personal space or the frequency of communication. In friendships, you may need to establish limits on how much emotional labor you are willing to take on, especially if a friend tends to vent or unload their problems with you often. With family, especially if you have a close-knit or demanding family, boundaries are essential for protecting your autonomy and ensuring that you are not overextending yourself.

How to Set Boundaries in Personal Relationships:

1. Identify Your Limits: Reflect on what makes you uncomfortable or stressed in your relationships. Where do you feel overextended or disrespected?
2. Communicate Clearly and Directly: Let the other person know your boundaries in a calm and respectful manner. Use "I" statements to

"Avoid power point blindness, where you can't see that the speaker is talking about you."

express how you feel, such as "I need time for myself after work" or "I feel uncomfortable when our conversations get too heated."

3. Be Consistent: Once you have set a boundary, it is important to stick to it. Inconsistency can confuse others and weaken the boundary you have established.

4. Prepare for Pushback: Some people may not immediately accept your boundaries, especially if they are used to a certain dynamic. Be prepared to hold firm, even if it feels uncomfortable at first.

5. Prioritize Your Mental Health: Remember that your well-being is just as important as anyone else's. Do not feel guilty about protecting your peace.

Teaching People How to Treat You

You must begin every relationship by teaching people how to treat you. If you want to be treated with respect and dignity you must demand respect and dignity from those with whomever you interact with. This does not have to be a negative interaction, but it does have to be one that fully reinforces your position. If you allow people to continually step on your toe and you say nothing; they will continue to step on your toe and will ultimately go further in their disrespect for you. It is important in both business and personal relationships that you attain and retain the respect that you deserve as a person, business partner or friend. One key to this is to be willing to give the same level of respect, concern, and human decency to others that you expect from them.

Remember, we teach people in our relationships with what we will and will not accept. We also learn from them what they will and will not accept from us. Unfortunately, we tend to give them what they expect and allow; not what they deserve as fellow compassionate human beings. This is another circumstance where we must steer away from our natural human tendencies and be better. The result is usually better relationships, stronger human bonds, better friendships, better love relationships and business relationships. In business, grow the business instead of creating internal strife and discord. Teaching people how to treat you is an essential aspect of time management, both in personal and professional relationships. If you allow others to

"Avoid power point blindness, where you can't see that the speaker is talking about you."

disrespect you, you'll find yourself spending a disproportionate amount of time dealing with unnecessary conflicts, misunderstandings, and emotional drain. On the other hand, when you set clear boundaries and expectations, you save time and energy that can be redirected toward more productive and meaningful activities.

Time management in this context involves recognizing the importance of boundaries early in relationships. Setting boundaries does not have to be confrontational, but it does have to be consistent. If you allow small acts of disrespect or disregard for your time to go unchecked, those behaviors will grow, and you will find yourself spending more time dealing with their consequences. For instance, if someone constantly interrupts your work or personal time with demands or unnecessary requests, and you do not address them, they will continue, eroding the time you could have spent on tasks that matter to you.

By teaching others how to respect your time and space, you also teach them to value their own. When

"Avoid power point blindness, where you can't see that the speaker is talking about you."

mutual respect is established, both parties are more likely to manage their interactions efficiently, saving time for everyone involved. In business, for example, a boss who respects an employee's time will receive better productivity because that employee won't feel the need to guard their time defensively or engage in passive-aggressive behaviors. Similarly, in personal relationships, clear expectations reduce the time wasted on misunderstandings and emotional fatigue, freeing both parties to enjoy their time together more fully.

In essence, effective time management starts with how you allow others to interact with you. Setting boundaries early and consistently ensures that your time is respected and valued, allowing you to focus on the things that truly matter.

"Avoid power point blindness, where you can't see that the speaker is talking about you."

Boundaries in Work Relationships *Workplace boundaries are just as crucial as personal boundaries, if not more so, because they directly affect your productivity, job satisfaction, and mental health. Without clear professional boundaries, it is easy to fall into patterns of overworking, saying "yes" to every task, or allowing coworkers or bosses to invade your personal time.*

For example, if you are constantly answering work emails after hours or agreeing to take on extra projects when your plate is already full, you may suddenly feel overwhelmed and resentful. Establishing clear boundaries in the workplace ensures that you maintain a healthy work-life balance and avoid burning out.

How to Set Boundaries at Work:

1. Define Your Work Hours: If you are constantly working outside of your set hours, it can blur the line between your professional and personal life. Communicate your availability to your team and stick to your designated work hours as much as possible.

"Avoid power point blindness, where you can't see that the speaker is talking about you."

2. Manage Expectations: Be clear with your boss or coworkers about what you can and cannot take on. If you are overloaded, do not be afraid to say, "I can't take on this project right now, but I can revisit it next week."
3. Delegate When Possible: If you are in a position where delegation is possible, make sure to use it. Taking on every task yourself can lead to burnout.
4. Protect Your Personal Time: Just because you are working from home or have access to work emails on your phone does not mean you should always be available. Set boundaries around your personal time and make sure to disconnect after work.
5. Have Difficult Conversations: If you feel that someone is overstepping your boundaries at work, whether it is a colleague or a supervisor, it is important to address it directly. While these conversations can be uncomfortable, they are necessary to support healthy professional relationships.

"Avoid power point blindness, where you can't see that the speaker is talking about you."

Boundaries and Time Management: Protecting Your Most Valuable Resource

Setting boundaries is one of the most effective tools for managing your time. Time is a finite resource, and without boundaries, it is easy for others to consume your time with their needs and demands, leaving you with little time for yourself or the things that truly matter to you.

Whether in your personal or professional life, setting boundaries helps you take control of your schedule, prioritize your responsibilities, and avoid the constant feeling of being "too busy." When you have clear limits in place, you are less likely to overcommit or feel pressured to say "yes" to everything, this allows you to focus on what is most important.

How Boundaries Improve Time Management:

1. Prioritizing Your Own Needs: When you set boundaries, you learn to prioritize what is important to you. Whether it is personal time, family commitments, or self-care, boundaries

"Avoid power point blindness, where you can't see that the speaker is talking about you."

ensure that your needs come first, which helps you manage your time more effectively.

2. Avoiding Overcommitment: Without boundaries, it is easy to say "yes" to every request, whether it is from friends, family, or coworkers. This can quickly lead to an overloaded schedule and stress. By setting boundaries, you can respectfully decline or postpone tasks that do not align with your priorities.

3. Creating Structure and Routine: Boundaries help create structure in your day. For instance, setting boundaries around work hours ensures that you're not constantly working overtime, giving you more time for personal interests, relaxation, and other critical areas of your life.

4. Reducing Distractions: Boundaries help you minimize distractions by establishing clear expectations with others. If you are working on an important project, for example, you can set boundaries with coworkers about when you are available for meetings or phone calls, allowing you to stay focused and productive.

"Avoid power point blindness, where you can't see that the speaker is talking about you."

5. **Improving Decision-Making:** With clear boundaries, decision-making becomes easier. You are more likely to make choices based on your values and priorities rather than out of guilt or obligation. This not only helps manage your time but also reduces stress and regret.

Practical Tips for Setting Time Boundaries:

- Learn to Say "No": Saying "no" can be difficult, especially if you are used to being a people-pleaser. However, declining requests that do not align with your priorities is essential for protecting your time. Practice saying "no" kindly but firmly.
- Set Time Limits: For activities that tend to consume more time than necessary (like meetings or phone calls), establish a clear time limit upfront. This helps keep conversations or tasks focused and ensures you have time for other responsibilities.
- Schedule Personal Time: Be available for yourself as a priority by scheduling it into

your calendar. Whether it's time for exercise, hobbies, or relaxation, treat it as non-negotiable.

- Communicate Your Availability: Let others know when you are available and when you are not. For example, if you do not want to answer work emails on weekends, communicate that boundary with your team.

By setting boundaries around your time, you reclaim control over your schedule and can better focus on the things that matter most to you—whether that is work, family, self-care, or personal growth.

"Avoid power point blindness, where you can't see that the speaker is talking about you."

Chapter: 23

Recognize That You are Telling a Story That Can Be Changed.

Remember each life is an ever-changing story, and you are in control of your story. Whether you like it or not, you are in charge unless you give your power away to others.

Make yourself the hero.

Remember you are the hero when you can achieve forgiveness. You are your own hero because you have enhanced your life, and you have given yourself back the peace of mind that another person has taken from you.

Being the hero of your story is a powerful metaphor for taking charge of your time and your life. In the context of time management, being the hero means that you are proactive rather than reactive. You understand that how you spend your time is ultimately a reflection of your priorities, and if you want to be the hero of your life, you need to invest time in the things that matter most to you.

"I am glad God doesn't have a three-strike rule."

Being the hero also means that you take responsibility for your time. Heroes do not wait for others to fix their problems or create opportunities for them; they actively seek out solutions and make the most of the time they have. They do not allow external circumstances to dictate their narrative. In terms of practical time management, this means setting boundaries, prioritizing tasks, and eliminating time-wasting activities that do not serve your personal story.

Legacy

Be careful of the legacy you leave for your children and those who know and love you.

This ties in close with the last section of the previous discussion. In the last section it recommends that you should never plan to leave a legacy of negative emotions that may flow through your family. In my last example from the last section this would be exactly what we are doing. For the smaller families this is an even more unhappy place to be, but equally hurtful no matter what size the family. I would much rather leave a legacy of love and caring than hate, distrust, and animosity; but not being in control is part of the human equation. You are only in charge

"I am glad God doesn't have a three-strike rule."

of what you can control. When dealing with a group of others, especially family, control is one thing you do not have. This is a situation where an agreement to begin, and a desire to reach a good endpoint, is desired by all, no matter how tedious and painful the conversation is.

Time is one of the most precious resources we have and understanding how we manage it can directly influence how our story unfolds. Each of us is telling a story through our actions, decisions, and behaviors. The beauty of this concept is that, just as a writer can edit or change their narrative, we too have the power to rewrite our personal stories. This directly relates to time management because every decision we make regarding how we spend our time contributes to the storyline we are creating for ourselves.

To take control of your time is to take control of your story. When you do not manage your time effectively, you risk giving away your power to external forces—allowing others, distractions, or even procrastination to control your narrative. But when you consciously decide how to use your time—whether it is working toward personal goals, investing in relationships, or

"I am glad God doesn't have a three-strike rule."

focusing on self-care—you actively steer your story in the direction you want it to go.

In this sense, time management becomes more than just organizing your day; it becomes a vital tool for shaping the kind of life you want to live. If you are constantly saying, "I don't have time," or "Life is out of my control," you are surrendering your ability to direct your story. Recognize that by taking charge of your time, you are reclaiming the ability to change the plot, the characters, and even the outcome. Just as a good author revise drafts to get the perfect ending, you too can revise your time allocation and habits to ensure your story reflects the life you want to lead.

Your Name

What is your name? Someone once said that we pass through life with at least three names; the name our parents give us, the name others give us and the name our reputation applies to us. A great and famous book that I love The Holy Bible King James Version, states; that a "good name is worth more than silver and gold." I have found this to be true and that is why I work to have a reputation that I can feel good about. The name that our parents have given us provides us

"I am glad God doesn't have a three-strike rule."

with our start and a place in the world. This name gives us a connection to others. The names friends and others give us can also have many meanings. Sometimes a tall person is called shorty or a person with red hair is called red. A person who is fast may be called speedy. Some of these names stick and are somewhat endearing, others can stick and are not endearing but survivable. Many of us even choose a different name because we do not like the name we were given. We will change the spelling or even create an entirely new name and persona. It is amazing the amount of time that is spent using a person's name. It is spoken, it appears on applications of all kinds, passports, credit applications, membership applications to churches, clubs, fraternities, sororities, civic clubs, and it is attached to your social security number. One of the most interesting name changes to me is when the singer Prince changed his name to a symbol. I would be very interested in how much time is spent regarding choosing names in our culture.

In my opinion, the most important name you have, however, is the name your reputation gives you. It is more about how people who know you feel when

"I am glad God doesn't have a three-strike rule."

your name is mentioned. Do they respect you as a person of ethics, and morals, a person who stands by their word? On the other hand, do they hear your name and feel the opposite way about you? Do they see you coming and want to go the other way? Are you trusted, hated, feared, respected, honored? It's really something to think about. I have heard people say that they do not care what other people think of them. That is when I really know they have clearly missed the boat regarding what this world is about and how we should really interact with one another. Perhaps there are those who really do not care what other people think, I'm not sure but isn't it the fact that you even mentioned the fact that not caring is an indication of some form of caring?

I suggest you try to have a good name. Live your life in a way that causes others to at least respect your name. It is important not only for you, but for your children and your family. It is not fair but, unfortunately, the stains of a bad name can move through generations. Is your name and reputation associated with saving time? I suggest having this because a person with an honored name and reputation can easily get things done. People will follow them and adhere to the principles they observe. It is important that influential people lead by reputation and action, not only by positional authority. I don't mean to belittle positional authority or indicate that it is okay to disrespect authority; but gaining discretionary effort from a team requires much more than positional authority. Discretionary effort requires that people feel you genuinely care. Your name and reputation as well as your day-to-day actions mean a lot to people and affect how they act, react, and provide services as well as completing their work each day. Your name, and more specifically your reputation, is intertwined with how efficiently you can manage your time. A good reputation opens doors and streamlines processes, while a poor one can lead to endless time spent cleaning up messes or repairing relationships. In personal and professional contexts, your name carries weight, and how people perceive it affects how they interact with you. If you are known for being reliable and ethical, people are more likely to trust you, follow through on commitments, and work efficiently with you.

Relating this to time management, consider the time saved when you do not have to prove yourself

"I am glad God doesn't have a three-strike rule."

repeatedly. A compelling reputation allows for smoother interactions, quicker decisions, and more productive collaborations. For example, in a business setting, someone with a good reputation can negotiate deals faster, manage teams more effectively, and avoid micromanagement because their word is trusted. Time is not wasted on second-guessing or unnecessary oversight. On the other hand, a poor reputation can lead to delays, as others may hesitate to work with you or demand extra assurances.

In your personal life, your name affects your relationships and how you manage your time with family, friends, and community. If people know you as someone who keeps promises and respects others' time, they are more likely to reciprocate. This leads to healthier, more efficient relationships, where time is not spent resolving conflicts or repairing damaged trust. In short, managing your name and reputation is a crucial element of time management. The effort you invest in maintaining a good reputation pays off in time saved. In the long run, you will face fewer obstacles and experience smoother, more respectful interactions with others

"I am glad God doesn't have a three-strike rule."

Chapter: 24

Decide

Decision-making is at the heart of effective time management. Every decision you make determines how your future unfolds. The concept of deciding whether to continue or end relationships, as highlighted in Chapter 23, parallels how we must make decisions about where we invest our time. The same applies to the fact that not every person can remain in our lives, not every task, commitment, or activity deserves a place in our schedule.

Time management is about making conscious decisions to either invest in something or let it go. Some tasks or relationships may have been important at one stage of life but no longer serve your growth. When you fail to decide—whether in relationships or time management—you are essentially allowing the problem to linger, draining your time and energy. Decisiveness allows you to move forward, allocate your time wisely, and focus on what truly matters.

When it comes to managing time, one of the most important decisions you can make is recognizing

"If you are not making any mistakes, it's quite possible you are not doing anything."

what is worth your time and what is not. This requires self-awareness and sometimes painful honesty. Not all opportunities are worth pursuing, and not all relationships are worth maintaining. Just as the previous text discussed the importance of deciding whether to continue or move on from a relationship, effective time management involves deciding which tasks, commitments, and whether or not the goals align with your values and priorities.

Not every person we want in our lives can continue to be a part of our lives no matter how bad we want it. Some hurts are so enduring that some people just cannot get past them and none of the strategies that I have mentioned in previous chapters will even scratch the surface in causing change in the feelings of the affected parties. The saddest part of this truth is that neither side in my life has wanted the situation to end the way it has, but time has left what we all call an indelible mark.

In this situation the parties have or will decide whether to continue without the relationship, rather than to try any further. My estimation of this is that

"If you are not making any mistakes, it's quite possible you are not doing anything."

in the saddest of situations, there is hope if all parties are willing to come together with a third-party control person who is not vested in the relationship with either party. This may result in a successful conversation.

This meeting needs one person who can bring the two groups together with the third party or is willing and able to bring the others together with the third-party control person to start the conversation. Most people are so involved in their own lives that even this may be a difficult proposition. It is worth a try even in the most difficult situations, but each person must decide if they care enough after years of failed relations, that it is worth the effort. I speak on this as I am currently embroiled in such a difficult situation, and I am not sure where it will finally land. It makes me sad on many levels, and I pray that a solution exists, but only the future will tell us if this happens… One thing I do know is that one way or the other whether we move forward together or move forward apart. I love them, and I pray they love me. I will deal with the hole in my life the best way I can, but I will not let it control,

"If you are not making any mistakes, it's quite possible you are not doing anything."

diminish, or damage my future life. I forgive them and I hope they forgive me but, we must all move on...

Your future can be as promising as you choose to make it. It takes work, perseverance, and a mind that forces the universe to work with them instead of against them. Living in the past is one of the most time-consuming and counterproductive habits we can develop. It is natural to reflect on our past decisions, but when we allow them to dominate our thoughts and actions, we waste the present and jeopardize our future. Whether it is missed opportunities, bad decisions, or failed ventures, dwelling on "what ifs" is a monument to nothingness. The past, no matter how important, is unchangeable. What is essential is recognizing how our past shapes us without letting it dictate how we manage our time moving forward.

Time management in this context means learning to let go. Worrying about the past robs us of time that could be spent planning, building, and creating a better future. If you spend hours lamenting over

"If you are not making any mistakes, it's quite possible you are not doing anything."

decisions that cannot be undone, you have forfeited the time you could have used to make positive changes. The time spent in regret is time lost forever. On the other hand, using the past as a reference point for learning, but not an anchor, allows us to manage our present more effectively. It frees us from mental clutter and enables us to take meaningful action toward our goals.

Moreover, as George Santayana also said, "Those who fail to learn from history are doomed to repeat it." This principle applies not only to global history but to our personal lives. Reflecting on mistakes with a constructive mindset can help us avoid repeating them. However, the key is balance. Time spent on reflection should lead to action, not paralysis. For example, if you missed out on starting a business because of fear, rather than dwelling on that lost opportunity, manage your time by planning a new venture, seeking advice, or learning the skills necessary to succeed. Each hour spent in constructive planning moves you forward, while hours spent in regret pull you backward. A well-

"If you are not making any mistakes, it's quite possible you are not doing anything."

managed life makes room for reflection but focuses on action

> "If you are not making any mistakes, it's quite possible you are not doing anything."

Chapter: 25

Thankfulness and Other Personal Ideas…

Everyone has something to be thankful for. Even the poorest, seemingly life lost person you come across has something to be thankful for. We must first as humans decide that other people's lot in life and our lot in life is only the beginning, a starting point toward a future of success or failure that we create. It is remarkably easy to be unhappy about our lot in life and find things to be unhappy about. This can lead to depression and rob your life of time and attention to the beautiful details in your life. Depression and sadness are a slippery slope that allow you to start downward; and as you start, it increases your slide until you feel as if you cannot stop it. One key to avoiding depression and extreme sadness is thankfulness. Each day of your life try to find something to be thankful for. Thankfulness is a powerful antidote to dissatisfaction and a key factor in managing your time and mental energy. It is easy to fall into a pattern of focusing on what we lack, whether it is money, time, or opportunities. This mindset drains our emotional energy and, ultimately, our time. When you focus on gratitude, you shift your

"Success is rarely accidental. It usually requires hard work."

attention from what you do not have to what you do have, making it easier to manage both your time and your emotional state.

Time management, when connected to gratitude, involves prioritizing what is tremendously important. When you recognize the abundance in your life, even in small things, you become less likely to waste time on trivial pursuits or negative thinking. Every moment spent in appreciation is a moment gained in mental clarity and focus. For example, instead of wasting time complaining about minor inconveniences, you can use that time to acknowledge the good things happening in your life, which leads to a more positive mindset and productive use of time.

Furthermore, gratitude helps you avoid the slippery slope of depression and sadness, which can consume vast amounts of your time and energy. Depression often leads to procrastination, where time slips away as we become engulfed in negative thoughts. However, by making a conscious effort to be thankful for even the smallest things, you can pull yourself out of that cycle and regain control over your time. This does not mean ignoring challenges or

"Success is rarely accidental. It usually requires hard work."

pretending everything is perfect. It means recognizing that, despite difficulties, there is always something worth appreciating. That simple shift in perspective can make a significant difference in how you spend your time, allowing you to focus on solutions instead of problems.

We Cannot Continue to Punish Ourselves for the Lessons Learned

Living in the past is one of the most time-consuming and counterproductive habits we can develop. It is natural to reflect on our past decisions, but when we allow them to dominate our thoughts and actions, we waste the present and jeopardize the future. Whether it is missed opportunities, bad decisions, or failed ventures, dwelling on "what ifs" is a "monument to nothingness." The past, no matter how important, is unchangeable. What is essential is recognizing how our past shapes us without letting it dictate how we manage our time moving forward. Time management in this context means learning to let go. Worrying about the past robs us of time that could be spent planning, building, and creating a better future. If you spend hours lamenting over decisions that cannot be

"Success is rarely accidental. It usually requires hard work."

undone, you have forfeited the time you could have used to make positive changes. The time spent in regret is time lost forever. On the other hand, using the past as a reference point for learning, but not an anchor, allows us to manage our present more effectively. It frees us from mental clutter and enables us to take meaningful action toward our goals.

The past tends to haunt us as we steer our lives toward the future. You must be very careful about allowing this to happen to you. What if I had gone to school? What if I had decided to have children? What if I had opened that business that I had always wanted to? Though these are interesting thoughts they are truly monuments to nothingness. No matter how much you worry about what you could have done in the past, you cannot change it. The past, good or bad, is etched in stone, unmovable, unchangeable and not something to dwell too deeply on.

The pursuit of wishful thinking of changes in your past can literally rob you of any time the future offers you. There is absolutely nothing anyone can do to erase, change, or rewrite our pasts. What you can do is abandon all hope for a better past and create, forge,

"Success is rarely accidental. It usually requires hard work."

plan, execute and begin a new and brighter future for yourself and those you love. This is not to say that the past is not important, it is these events that have shaped who we are in the present. Additionally, the adage stated by Frederick Douglass "those who forget the mistakes of the past are doomed to repeat them." This is true. This principle applies not just to global history but to our personal lives. Reflecting on mistakes with a constructive mindset can help us avoid repeating them. However, the key is balance. Time spent on reflection should lead to action, not paralysis. I have witnessed friends and family as well as myself, fail to learn from past mistakes; and have made the same mistakes repeatedly. Then, we sit and wonder "Why am I in the position that I am in?" The goal is to not let past mistakes or successes rule your future.

For example, if you missed out on starting a business because of fear, rather than dwelling on that lost opportunity, manage your time by planning a new venture, seeking advice, or learning the skills necessary to succeed. Each hour spent in constructive planning moves you forward, while hours spent in regret pull you backward. A well-

"Success is rarely accidental. It usually requires hard work."

managed life makes room for reflection but focuses on action. A great business example would be the slow and agonizing death of Sears Roebuck and Company. This company went from being one, if not, the biggest retailer in the modern world, to almost non-existent today. Then other players entered the game, Walmart, Target, and Amazon. These retailers entered the market with new ideas and business plans and had nowhere near the capital that Sears had and was able to overtake them; and would soon put them completely out of business. Many baby boomers remember the Sears catalog and eagerly wait to look through and pick what they wanted. You could get almost anything from Sears including cars and homes. Walmart found the chink in their armor and utilized it to slowly and methodically overtake them. Sears believed that what worked for them in the past would work for them in the future and refused to make changes swiftly enough to compensate. I do not want this for you, or anyone; so, use the past for what it is, a guide and a reference tool to learn from but not as a place to rest all your sadness.

"Success is rarely accidental. It usually requires hard work."

Change and Growth

Being better only requires trying to be better. A desire to leave your old life behind and begin a new and better way of doing things begins with a simple conscious decision to move forward and not backward in your actions and your thinking. Moving forward in your actions is not as difficult a proposition as changing and altering one's mindset. A person's mindset develops over time and the more years you have behind you the more set in your ways and rigid your thinking can become. Using myself for example, years ago I would never have seen myself being accepted in the world we live in today. A world where the pronouns he/she for some groups are replaced with them and they, in direct contradiction with what my eyes and ears are showing and telling me. Luckily, being in the HR field and having millennial children has helped me manage and change with the times and not only accept the new communities and all their variations but to embrace and understand the need for change. This is so true in the workplace, where change is sometimes more difficult. We live in a workplace society where in the past, the term breast feeding could be considered offensive to some people. Therefore, some companies have altered the terminology to chest feeding. Traditional men's and women's restrooms have taken on a new meaning in many workplaces. Individuals who see themselves as a female even though they are male by gender may use the traditional female restroom and vice versa for an individual who presents as female but is transitioning to become male, may use the male facilities. Society must evolve with the times, and each generation must make room for the morals and differences of the next one. Organizations sometimes find this kind of change very disconcerting, unsettling and difficult. That is why it is important not only to have a diverse employee base; but one that is generationally diverse as well as culturally diverse with sensitivity to race, gender, nationality, and orientation concerns.

In the most difficult situations, training is needed throughout the organization, not just to avoid litigation, but to enhance the worker experience which directly impacts customer and stakeholder outcomes. Cultural change is very difficult in some organizations, and it may take some time and energy to achieve it, but it is well worth it to turn the corner

"Success is rarely accidental. It usually requires hard work."

in many organizations.

Happiness

Happiness can be a fleeting and a seemingly unattainable goal for many people. We usually do not realize how much control we have over our thinking. We may not have control over our finances, an individual's reaction toward us, community, family, or national events; but we do have control over our reaction to events that affect our state of mind. The internet is rife with strategies that may help us with the issue of our happiness, but in using any of these; remember you or your state of mind are the key. The following are some strategies that I have found in my searches, that will help you create some sustainable happiness. First, connect socially. Most human beings are social creatures, and we desire to interact with others. This is as different for each of us as there are people on the planet; but think about how many of our activities involve large groups of people. Sporting events, reunions, parties, bar hops, cruises, and so, simply spending time with family and friends can be one of the most influential things you can do to be happy and create a good work life balance. Be mindful; and appreciate the moment that you are in because it will never come again. Secondly, the future is uncertain, and the past is unchangeable so meditate on the positive and beautiful things in the current moment in time. For example, the beauty of a butterfly, the sounds of the wind blowing through the trees, a baby cooing. Find time in your day to concentrate on the good things that life has to offer, and what you have right at your fingertips. The third strategy I like is to become more active. Health and physical activity go hand in hand. A proper diet and regular exercise can increase and produce hormones in your brain that enhance feelings of happiness. Start slowly and work your way into any exercise program so that you do not injure yourself. Speak with your doctor on your best dietary path and stick to it as best you can. You do not have to give up everything you like, but moderation is the key. The next key to happiness is difficult for some. I understand that; but it is the one that I will include here. Be spiritual. Notice that I said "spiritual," not religious. Some form of spirituality, no matter what your belief is or the lack thereof, offers a foundation for happiness.

Use your finances wisely, expenditure on experiences can bring much more gratification than

"Success is rarely accidental. It usually requires hard work."

the short-term pleasure of an expensive purchase that very soon has no meaning. Activities with friends, family, significant other, and/or a retreat with like-minded people can be very rewarding.

Be resilient. we all get knocked down in our journey through life. However, it does not matter how many times you get knocked down. What matters is how many times you get up. Every success is getting up one more time than you were knocked down. No one likes adversity, we all hate it, and we all want everything to go our way. We always think we should have gotten the job, the promotion or whatever. That is not how life works, and it never will be. There will be good times, and there will be troubled times, and the way we plan and react or go about our lives, generally decides the amount of adversity we will have and how we will react to it.

Give thanks. Happiness and gratitude are inexorably linked. I was speaking with someone the other day and they really did not believe in the happiness mantra I was spewing, so I asked them to change their perspective just for a moment. They asked what I meant, and I said, "Let's say you just bought a new car and had a horrible accident. However, you and

"Success is rarely accidental. It usually requires hard work."

your wife and child are fine. In that situation, concentrate on the fact that you, your wife, and your child were not injured instead of the fact your new car was totaled." Yes, it is bad that your car is destroyed, and you must deal with the insurance agents and get a new car but, in the grand scheme of things, be grateful that your family survived. You can find good in the most terrible times of your life if you look back, even if it is just the fact that you survived it and lived to fight another day. Every day try to find a moment to think of the things for which you are grateful and write them down. It is a very interesting exercise.

Be positive. This is a hard one in a shattered world like the one we live in. Smiling and engaging in positive non-destructive behaviors can help you become more positive even if it is not how you initially feel. Have you ever had someone just smile at you and it improved your mood? You smiled back even though you weren't at your best. A simple smile can be contagious. During our masked society of COVID 19, the one thing I miss is the occasional smiling faces.

Live a meaningful life. Find joy in your journey or

find a path you can enjoy. Have goals and aspirations that have meaning for you that will help others. When I chose to help another person, it did in most, if not all, circumstances, enrich my life. It let me know that my journey is not only about me. It's about all of us and how we are connected.

There are several parts to the happiness equation and its definition. There is short term happiness, this type of happiness is caused by humor in all its many various facets, whether its music, movies, shows or internet searches. It can also be a pleasant surprise, like a call from a friend you have not heard from in a while. It also includes pleasures of all kinds like food, sex, and relaxation.

Next, there is long term happiness which is characterized by the meaning and purpose that you have in your life. This includes feelings of fulfillment which some call success, and inspiration that guides us to succeed and be better than we think we can be. Most important to me is a lasting love. This is especially true with one that you can count on through thick and thin, through good times and even more so during troubled times.

Your mind helps control your state of happiness

"Success is rarely accidental. It usually requires hard work."

based on your beliefs, your mental habits, and your attitude towards both success and adversity along with your ability to attain and maintain a positive focus.

The last part of the equation is your body. As I have discussed before, your state of health, and what you do to improve or diminish it; whether you engage in physical activity or not, having positive daily habits enhances your life and the lives of the people around you. Lastly, how you maintain a high energy level either through proper diet or vitamins and proper medical care enhances your happiness factor.

> "Success is rarely accidental. It usually requires hard work."

Chapter: 26

Race, Ethnicity, Gender, Sexual Orientation and Use of Time

Race, ethnicity, gender, and sexual orientation significantly shape how people use their time in both social and professional situations when faced with cultural expectations. These factors influence an individual's roles within peer groups, households, communities, and workplaces, leading to differences in time spent on paid work, household responsibilities, and leisure activities.

Here are some of the keys these factors intersect with time use:

Race and Ethnicity

Labor Market Participation: It is a known fact whether people acknowledge it or not, that people from specific racial and ethnic backgrounds often face disparities in employment opportunities and wage gaps. For example, Black and Hispanic individuals may work longer hours in lower-paying jobs, which affects their time for rest, leisure, or household responsibilities. Promotional

"How many people do you know that you can give a blank check to?"

opportunities and other workplace benefits can be tempered by institutional and unintentional biases that people harbor against other groups based on stereotypes that have been shown in all the forms of media and passed along as fact by peers, coworkers, and family members.

Cultural Expectations: Cultural norms within racial and ethnic communities can also dictate how time is allocated. For instance, extended family obligations may lead some racial or ethnic groups to spend more time on caregiving or family activities. Not only does the cultural factor appear here, but the fact that they are paid less for their time causes these groups to have to make decisions that their counterparts in other groups can solve by their financial position in life.

Work Schedules: In some cases, racial and ethnic minorities might be overrepresented in industries with non-traditional work schedules (e.g., night shifts or weekend work), which can affect their overall time use patterns, especially regarding family and leisure time. This can also impact sleep schedules, and overall health, and access to health care.

"How many people do you know that you can give a blank check to?"

Compounded Effects: The intersection of race, ethnicity, and gender often exacerbates time use disparities. For instance, women of color may face a dual burden of discrimination in the workplace along with expectations to manage most household duties. This can leave them with less time for personal leisure, career advancement, or self-care compared to men or women from more privileged racial or ethnic groups.

Impact of Socioeconomic Status

These factors are also influenced by socioeconomic status, where marginalized groups may need to work multiple jobs or longer hours due to financial constraints. This can further limit the time available for leisure, self-development, and family life.

In essence, race, ethnicity, and gender shape not just the opportunities people have, but how they manage their daily lives and time resources. The cumulative effect of these identities can reinforce social inequalities, particularly in access to leisure, work-life balance, and economic mobility.

"How many people do you know that you can give a blank check to?"

Gender

Work and Home Life: Compared to men, even though in the recent century women have gained positions in the workplace in various levels of advancement, regardless of their race or ethnicity, they also tend to spend an inordinate amount of time on valuable but unpaid labor (household chores, child rearing and caregiving) compared to men. Men, on average, devote more time to paid work. However, the number of men that are now moving to the position of house husband has increased dramatically. There are many examples where this arrangement works well depending on the attitudes and upbringing of the couples involved. However, in my close-knit group I am aware of a couple of situations that fit into this category that lasted several years but ended poorly. The blame should not be placed on the people involved. The dissolution of the marriages could have happened even if they had chosen a different home make up.

Leisure Time: Men often have more leisure time than women, particularly when factoring in unpaid domestic responsibilities. There is some truth to the fact that some of the leisure activities that men engage in are used as mechanisms for career progression. Consider Golf as an example: It is often mentioned that a lot of large-scale deals and promotion discussions are made on the golf course, or tennis court etc.

Workplace Roles: Until very recently in the workplace, gender in the workplace has led to men and women occupying different roles, which might dictate their work hours or flexibility, influencing how much time is left for other activities. Specifically, many women in the past were relegated to secretarial roles or other similar roles that were at that time considered acceptable female positions. This has changed somewhat, but the gap has yet to close sufficiently to consider the issue closed. Women's pay, for example in many cases, still lags men's pay in the same or similar roles.

Sexual orientation Sexual orientation can influence time management, largely through its interaction with social expectations, workplace dynamics, and family structures. While research on this topic is growing, there are several ways in which sexual orientation might have an impact on how individuals manage their time:

"How many people do you know that you can give a blank check to?"

Everyone has everything in their family …

Humans have the tendency to want to feel that they are better than others. In my sixty plus years on this planet I have met rich and poor and everyone in between and one thing I have noticed is that most families regardless of their station in life, all have the same things existing in their families, if they are honest with themselves. We all have someone who made a bad decision and went to jail or should have; a person who has been down the path of drug abuse both legally and illegally, or a person who overindulges in alcohol. Some have alternative lifestyles in the family, some rich, some poor and middle-income, even highly educated and those with little or no education. Some who are wise, some who are not so wise whether educated or not; and some who are physically gifted and some that are not gifted. So, are we as different as we think we are if a little of everything exists in almost every family? Why are we surprised when we find out about Cousin Bob living in the basement or Auntie Sara marrying Patricia? The world is complex, and each family is part of that complexity. The diversity and strangeness of an experience, if viewed correctly, can really enhance our

"How many people do you know that you can give a blank check to?"

lives instead of diminishing them.

Though our viewpoints and acceptance of certain behaviors may be different, it does not allow us to love anyone any less or treat them any worse. It's quite the opposite; we should treat them better, love them more, and pray for all without ceasing. When we examine our families, it becomes clear that everyone has a mixture of people and experiences that reflect the complexity of the human condition. Some individuals may have been involved in less-than-ideal situations, like drug abuse, alcohol overindulgence, or even time in prison. Others may have achieved significant success, wealth, or advanced education. Yet, despite these differences, there is a remarkable sameness across all families.

Relating this to time management, it is important to realize that these family dynamics—whether positive or negative—take up our time and energy. We often find ourselves consumed by the actions of others in our families, whether it is worrying about a loved one's poor decisions or feeling joy over someone's success. Time management here means learning to compartmentalize and balance the emotional energy spent on family issues. It is easy to spend time judging

"How many people do you know that you can give a blank check to?"

or reacting to these situations, but is that time spent effectively? When we acknowledge that every family has its challenges, we can become more accepting, less judgmental, and free up emotional energy to focus on what we can control—our own time, actions, and future.

Moreover, understanding the universal nature of these issues can help us avoid being blindsided by life's complexities. Instead of being shocked or stressed about family difficulties, we can prepare ourselves to manage our time and emotional resources better. For example, instead of spending hours in reactive states of mind, we can use that time to develop strategies to handle family matters in a productive and loving way. Learning to embrace family diversity and unpredictability can ultimately enhance how we manage our time, allowing us to respond thoughtfully rather than react impulsively. It also helps us focus on the things we can influence, like nurturing better relationships and spending our time wisely on personal growth.

Chosen Family: LGBTQ+ individuals often place significant value on "chosen families" (supportive

"How many people do you know that you can give a blank check to?"

friends and community members) and may spend more time cultivating these relationships, especially if estranged from biological family due to their sexual orientation. It is wholly unfair that these groups find themselves ostracized from their birth families and for many years it seemed that this was more prevalent in the African American community.

Its fine for you to lead the choir on Sunday but do not "come out" on Monday. Many churches have even preached against the people that lead their choirs and other organizations in the church or worse refuse any recognition whatsoever. This causes individuals to attempt to hide in plain sight if they want to remain a member of the group, or become so disenchanted they leave their faith, organization, or group to find one that is more comfortable to exist in.

Leisure and Social Time

Social Networks: LGBTQ+ individuals might also spend time in LGBTQ-specific spaces (events, clubs, advocacy groups) to find acceptance and community, which can shape how they allocate their social and leisure time.

In summary, sexual orientation can shape time management through workplace experiences, family dynamics, social expectations, and personal well-being. LGBTQ+ individuals may face unique challenges or opportunities related to these factors, which can influence how they navigate their daily lives. It can be beneficial to any organization that they recognize and have a plan to work with these concerns within the bounds of current policy or create new policies that benefit both the individual and the institution.

Workplace Dynamics and Discrimination

LGBTQ+ Discrimination: LGBTQ+ individuals may face workplace discrimination or bias, which can affect job opportunities, promotions, and work hours. Navigating these challenges may require additional time and energy spent on job searching, proving competence, or dealing with stress from hostile work environments. This has recently become exacerbated by the general reducing of many companies' policies around inclusion. This is a nice way of saying "this country or company are no longer going to recognize this as an important aspect of our culture." This becomes problematic when this is who this group of people are, just the same as the mainstream group is who they are. Society may wonder if this is a way of saying some discrimination against some groups is now okay. Or are we reverting to past practice of discrimination? It sure seems that way.

Job Security and Time Allocation: Some LGBTQ+ individuals may avoid certain industries or workplaces where they fear discrimination, potentially leading to job instability, underemployment, or part-time work. This can affect how they balance paid work, personal time, and household responsibilities. Most organizations feel this is a personal decision not to fit in and therefore it's not the company's problem. I see it as a broader issue than that. We must ask ourselves if we are comfortable in creating a society where people that may be the best qualified and most talented will not even apply be because they know they will be treated unfairly because of their choice in clothing, hair color, or other such issues not directly related to job performance.

"How many people do you know that you can give a blank check to?"

Family Structures and Responsibilities

Non-Traditional Family Roles: Same-sex couples often have more fluid or non-traditional roles within the household, which can influence how they divide unpaid labor like childcare or housework. It must be common knowledge that same-sex couples, especially lesbian couples, tend to have more equitable divisions of labor than heterosexual couples. For a while businesses were more open to allocating time to support these nontraditional families but in 2024 this seems to be changing.

Parenting Time: LGBTQ+ parents might spend time navigating legal and social systems to secure parental rights, deal with stigma, or ensure the well-being of their children. These added responsibilities may take extra time compared to heterosexual parents.

Coming Out and Identity Management: LGBTQ+ individuals often dedicate a substantial amount of time, energy, and emotional labor to managing their identities across different areas of life—including family dynamics, professional environments, religious spaces, healthcare settings,

"How many people do you know that you can give a blank check to?"

and broader social communities. Coming out is not a one-time event but a continuous process that must often be revisited with each new relationship, job, doctor's visit, or public encounter. For many, this act of disclosure can be both empowering and burdensome, depending on the level of safety and support available in each setting.

In environments where acceptance is not guaranteed, identity management becomes a form of self-preservation. Individuals may have to constantly assess whether it is safe to disclose their gender identity or sexual orientation, weighing the risks of discrimination, social rejection, or even physical harm. This vigilance and emotional calculation can be mentally exhausting and often detracts from the time and energy that could be spent on work, relationships, or personal growth.

On a practical level, administrative and bureaucratic challenges can be overwhelming. For transgender and non-binary individuals, legal name and gender marker changes involve navigating a patchwork of local and state laws that may require court orders, notarized documents, publication in newspapers, and

"How many people do you know that you can give a blank check to?"

multiple appearances at government agencies. These procedures often come with financial costs and can take weeks or months to complete. In the workplace, updating employment records may require interactions with multiple departments—such as Human Resources, IT, payroll, and legal compliance—each step potentially exposing individuals to misgendering or misunderstanding.

Additionally, the emotional labor of educating others—coworkers, supervisors, family members, or service providers—can become a recurring responsibility that LGBTQ+ individuals are expected to take on, further adding to the invisible workload of managing one's identity. All of this together paints a picture of how the management of identity is not just personal but deeply structural, affecting time, mental health, access to resources, and the quality of everyday life.

Social and Emotional Labor

Community Engagement: LGBTQ+ individuals may spend more time engaged in advocacy, activism, or community-building activities, which can be a source of support but also an added time

"How many people do you know that you can give a blank check to?"

commitment compared to non-LGBTQ+ individuals. This can have a negative impact on their work lives since it will seem that they are less available than other employees and this creates hesitancy in management regarding promotional opportunities and other project-based assignments

"How many people do you know that you can give a blank check to?"

UNDERSTANDING AND USING TIME

Chapter: 27

Fluidity of Time

From a scientific perspective, time seems to move along at a constant and unchanging rate. But a human being's perspective of time changes this equation. Some of us remember as a child when mom and dad promised us a trip to Disney or to visit grandma, time seemed to crawl along, and it would take forever until the moment you left for the vacation or visit. Conversely, once you arrived time seemed to speed up, and the vacation or visit was over before you knew it. Similarly, have you traveled to a new destination for the first time, and it seemed to take forever to reach the location? However, when headed home or back to your original location the trip seemed somehow shorter, or it seemed that time moved along quicker. No one really believes that the flow of time changed in any way, however the feeling persists. So let us look at some of the factors that impact how we perceive and interact with time.

How we perceive time can vary depending on several psychological and situational factors. Here are a few key reasons why time may seem to pass slowly or quickly:

Attention and Engagement

Boredom can be a key factor in how you perceive and interact with time. When you are bored or not mentally engaged, time can seem to drag. This is because you are more aware of the passage of time, and there's little stimulation to distract your mind. In the current era, people use social media to reduce the boredom of everyday existence.

Flow State Introduced by Michaly Csikszentmihalyi in 1970, is interestingly, a relatively new term that means if you are engaged in an activity, then your feeling of how fast or slow time passes is affected. You specifically perceive that time is passing much faster. When you are deeply engaged in an activity you enjoy, you are less focused on the passing of time. This may be the reason that when you are on a fun-filled trip or vacation time seems to speed up.

Routine vs. Novelty

When individuals are involved in rote work or repetitive tasks, they become so engrossed in the task they are performing that they look up and the entire

"Why is it so easy to say no, and so hard to find a way to say yes?'

workday has passed. When you are in a routine, your brain becomes accustomed to the sameness, and as a result, time feels like it is passing quickly. Days can blur together when you are doing the same things repeatedly. But when a person starts new experiences, their brain must process more information, thus making time feel like it is slowing down. For example, a vacation in a new place can feel much longer than a typical workday. And at the same time, the elation and joy of the vacation can make time seem to speed up. This is an odd conundrum.

A person's emotional state has a huge bearing on how they interact with time. Stress, anxiety, happiness, and sadness can all directly affect the individual's perception of the passage of time. During stressful or anxiety-inducing situations, your perception of time can slow down. This is thought to be a survival mechanism, where the brain pays closer attention to detail, giving you more perceived time to react. We have all seen this displayed in movies when the person in the movie is under stress the director uses this moment to slow the action down. This is like what happens to an individual under stress.

"Why is it so easy to say no, and so hard to find a way to say yes?'

Happiness versus sadness, when you are happy or content, time often seems to fly by (as I mentioned earlier in the vacation example). Conversely, when you are sad or going through a difficult period, it can feel like time is dragging. We all have experienced the dark days in our lives when we felt that our problems were insurmountable, and the dark clouds would never disappear. For most people, these days are inordinately long, and while this is when we are in the "valley" parts of our lives we must be careful not to become overwhelmed and let the situation cause us to make extremely bad decisions.

As we age our perception of time changes. Possibly because we become more aware of our mortality. As we grow older, time tends to feel like it passes more quickly. This may be because a single year becomes a smaller fraction of our overall life experience and a bigger part of the remaining time that we think we have left. When you are a child, a year feels much longer because it is a larger part of your total life up to that point. Everything is new and the future seems so far away you wonder if you will ever reach it. Everything seems possible and probable.

"Why is it so easy to say no, and so hard to find a way to say yes?'

Another factor to consider is when we are in anticipation of a certain thing, event, or activity. Similarly, the feeling of delayed gratification or waiting for something, time can seem to slow down. The anticipation of a future event can make the present moment feel longer. For example, you got tickets to see your favorite performer when you were young. It seemed like decades before the date of the concert would arrive, but time moved along at the constant rate it always does.

These factors are connected to how your brain processes time based on internal and external stimuli.

Next, let us move to the nonscientific thoughts about time. Many, if not all of us, have dreams. In these dreams, which on average last no more than one hour to three hours of the eight hours that we remain asleep, can at times seem to last a lifetime. I have had dreams on several occasions, that cover years of time. I expect you have had the same experience. In this dream is time different? If it's not, then how is it possible to experience years in a heartbeat? The answer is still unknown, but scientists have tried to study it and come to conclusions about how this

"Why is it so easy to say no, and so hard to find a way to say yes?'

occurs. Most of them believe it is a trick that the brain plays on us. But in our minds, we are experiencing years in moments. The time that we dream is called REM, Rapid Eye Movement sleep. During this time, the brain becomes highly energized and active. It processes information in ways that are much different than when we are awake. This leads to a compression or expansion of time and its perception. Events that would take hours or days in real life can be condensed into seconds in a dream.

Since dreams do not unfold in real time as they do in waking time it is believed that the brain edits and may skip over unnecessary parts and may even jump between different scenes. If the brain has experienced some of the events, then the dreamers do not need the missed sections because they are already a part of the dreamer's memory core. This creates an illusion of experiencing days, months, or years in a brief period.

The other factor to consider is that when you are asleep and dreaming, your internal chronometer is no longer synchronized to the external or actual time cues. This makes time perception in dream time more subjective and malleable, creating the effect of

"Why is it so easy to say no, and so hard to find a way to say yes?'

experiencing long sequences of time in short moments. The combination of altered brain activity, narrative disassociation, and emotional factors allow a dreamer to experience time in an alternate fashion. Research has shown that this is a necessary part of the sleep cycle and many sleep scientists believe that all people dream and that it is a crucial factor in having a healthy mind. Now the correlation becomes clear that dreaming and experiencing time in this alternate fashion, is a principal factor in how we use and experience time.

"Why is it so easy to say no, and so hard to find a way to say yes?'

Chapter: 28

The "To Do List" and Time Management

I believe everyone has heard of, created, or been punished by the dread of a to do list. It is just a real-life agenda for everyday tasks that you either need to do, should do, or someone has asked or required you to do. The biggest problem with these lists is that most of the items that end up on your to-do list are things you would prefer not to do. Things like cutting and edging the grass, raking the leaves, cleaning the gutters, washing the clothes, going grocery shopping, cleaning a room, washing the dishes and many other mundane tasks that may need to be done but we would love to figure out a way to put them off as long as possible. Because of the nature of these tasks, people have even created businesses that make billions of dollars a year ridding us of these tasks. Lawn services, grocery delivery, housekeeping and cleaning services, fast food delivery services, and even shopping services like Stitch Fix to name a few. People will go to extreme lengths and great expense to avoid completing some of the needed and traditionally normal tasks that are a part of our everyday lives. This is justified by the time that's saved not having to do these tasks, the fact that they can afford them, and even the feeling that certain tasks are beneath them because of their station in life, or the feeling that they are creating jobs for others since they don't want to do these tasks. In all honesty, there is truth in the last part of that statement. Many jobs were created because one group or another, no longer wants to, must or needs to spend their time engaged in completing those tasks.

So, what if you have a to do list, and you are fully invested and have the time, or want to complete the tasks yourself? Whatever situation you find yourself in; what is the best and most economical way to go about checking off the items on your to-do list? I will say that this really depends on the person, the amount of time they have available, and the desire to complete tasks rather than a propensity to find excuses not to complete tasks. The fastest and most efficient way to reduce the number of items on your to-do list, is not to procrastinate. I discussed earlier how procrastination can affect time management. If any item on your list can be completed immediately and not cause you any problems or discomfort, go ahead and get it done. I received a package that I

"What's the most important part of the human body?"

ordered in the mail, and the retailer sent the wrong size. So instantly, my to do list had another item added to it, that also had a deadline. I put it to the side as just another issue to deal with later, but when I walked by it moments later, I realized that I had the time to do it at that very moment and it wouldn't take very long to return it where the retailer required me to, then, I could check off not only the return but a couple of other items on my list while doing it. By taking the initiative to do it this way, I completed not only the task that was added to my list but two other items in the process. The lesson here is that procrastination is not always in your best interest. Be aware that I am not saying to rush and do everything. There is some merit in waiting to make changes to your schedule or plans because I have found that some conflicts that arise on your schedule will resolve themselves, if you are patient, just don't allow being patient to become a situation where you fail to make the necessary decisions in your business and personal life. Once you have completed all the items on your "to-do list" that require little time, and do not have a deadline, it is time to move to those items that have increased time requirements and need to be

"What's the most important part of the human body?"

accomplished by a deadline. I would suggest putting those items in order by the deadline and time requirement, then working down the list until completion. Be aware that, as with any schedule, unplanned items can and will occur and must be managed, added, and removed from the list as they occur. The only thing that will torpedo completion is illness, procrastination, unexpected events, and failure to plan properly. An illness is unplanned and can cause the completion of your to do list to come to a screeching halt. This can be more than problematic for those who are entrepreneurs, because they are their business. This is also a problem for small or newly formed businesses as well. In most large businesses, there are alternative individuals that can aid or be required by management, to fill in the gaps so even though the illness is a concern, it is less of a concern in larger businesses. There are many unexpected events that can occur in your home, life, and in business. If you are working on a to-do list and your child is injured, then the injury becomes the only thing on your mind and takes precedence over everything else. In business, a CEO could unexpectedly retire, and a new one comes in with an

"What's the most important part of the human body?"

entirely new direction or added directives that can change how you move forward. The solution becomes clear that you should reassess the situation, reallocate your time and to-do list chronology and get started. The main idea here is focus, plan and not overreact to situations that affect your day.

"What's the most important part of the human body?"

Chapter: 29
Time and Specific Creations/Constructions

One of Michelangelo's greatest works of art is arguably the Sistine Chapel Ceiling, titled the Last Judgement. It is stated that the completion of this work took four years between 1536 and 1541. It is said that Michelangelo spent 18 hours a day working on the Sistine Chapel. Let us put this in perspective, 18 hours a day, 7 days a week over 4 years adds up to 26,208 hours of work. This is what I would call a tremendous use of time where the results have lasted from 1541 to now and we have no idea how long it will be preserved. In the movie, "The Agony and the Ecstasy," portraying the painting of the Sistine Chapel ceiling, it is said that Pope Julius II said, "when will you make an end?" Michelangelo retorts "When I am finished!" I am not sure that this movie indicates actual events, but it is not unreasonable that the Pope may have wanted the work completed quickly. What is more interesting is that Michelangelo was not going to let an arbitrary time parameter decide when his master work was completed. Each of us is an artist as well and we need to use the time

"Some people spend a lot of time and energy trying to avoid following the process or procedure, when they could be finished if they had followed them."

allotted to us wisely as we create our life masterpieces. I know art can be a bit esoteric and for some, a less concrete way to judge the use of time. So, let us consider the Hoover Dam project and the Panama Canal construction as more concrete examples of usage and expenditure of time.

The Hoover Dam Project is located along the Colorado River, between Arizona and Nevada, in the USA. Between 1900 and 1929, concerns about the Colorado River flooding, energy needs for the growing west, not to mention water conservation considerations; caused the U. S. government to consider the building of the dam. Regardless of cost and difficulty consideration, in 1929 President Herbert Hoover signed a bill into law that established the Boulder Canyon Project Act, which officially approved the dam's construction. The dam was constructed between 1931 and 1936 and began generating Hydroelectric power and still functions to this day. Approximately 5 years of construction at a cost of $49 million dollars which is equivalent to $700 million in today's dollars when adjusted for inflation. These costs are not as important as the loss of life

"Some people spend a lot of time and energy trying to avoid following the process or procedure, when they could be finished if they had followed them."

that was associated with the construction. Ninety-Six workers died during the construction of the Hoover Dam. The reasons were various, including heatstroke, falling debris, and drowning to name a few. Now let's consider the Panama Canal, located at the Isthmus of Panama, connecting the Atlantic and Pacific Oceans. The purpose was to decrease the travel time for ships by providing a shortcut instead of sailing around the southern tip of South America. The first attempt to build the canal was in 1881 by the French under the leadership of an engineer by the name of Ferdinand de Lesseps, the builder of the Suez Canal. The project faced massive challenges with tropical diseases, poor planning, and engineering difficulties. In 1889 the French effort collapsed due to bankruptcy and failure to solve the challenges posed by the dense jungle, tropical climate, and difficult terrain. During this time, 22,000 workers lost their lives. In 1903, after Panama declared independence from Columbia with US support, and the US signed the Hay-Buneau-Varilla treaty gaining rights to the Canal Zone. In 1904 the US officially took control of the canal project. Construction lasted from 1904-1914 when the canal opened to traffic and

"Some people spend a lot of time and energy trying to avoid following the process or procedure, when they could be finished if they had followed them."

is still considered one of the greatest engineering feats of its time. During the American construction 5,600 workers died, mostly from accidents and diseases like malaria and yellow fever. The final cost of the Panama Canal was about $375 million equivalent to about $10 billion in today's dollars when adjusted for inflation. Each project took inordinate amounts of time and resources. I mention this because most of the emphasis is usually centered on the financial costs of these projects. I consider time our most valuable resource for the reasons mentioned earlier. When you consider the amount of time and loss of life that these projects have caused, the perspective changes greatly. The time spent in many ways can be justified in that both projects are still in production and will continue to produce for years into the future. I believe most of us would spend a year getting to ten, so the justification is obvious. The loss of life, however, is a much different consideration and everyone must rationalize this for themselves.

In my humble opinion each of our lives is also a massive construction project like the Hoover Dam or the Panama Canal. We must decide daily, weekly,

"Some people spend a lot of time and energy trying to avoid following the process or procedure, when they could be finished if they had followed them."

monthly, and yearly if the time we plan to spend on each project, activity, or assignment is a valuable use of our most precious resource, the time allocated for our existence.

"Some people spend a lot of time and energy trying to avoid following the process or procedure, when they could be finished if they had followed them."

Chapter: 30

Time Management & Other Related Quotes

Here is a list of famous and not so famous quotes about time and time management. Some are from people you know and others that you may have never heard of.

- "We must use time as a tool, not as a couch." — **John F. Kennedy**
- "Time you enjoy wasting is not wasted time." — **Marthe Troly-Curtin**
- "Time is what we want most but what we use worst." — **William Penn**
- "Tough times never last, but tough people do." — **Robert H. Schuller**
- "'Someday' is a disease that will take your dreams to the grave with you." — **Timothy Ferriss**
- "Yesterday's the past, tomorrow's the future, but today is a gift. That's why it's called the present." — **Bil Keane**
- "Better three hours too soon than a minute too late." — **William Shakespeare**

"Concentrate on the things that matter in life. Money, fame, power and prestige are not on the top of the list."

- "The past always looks better than it was. It's only pleasant because it isn't here." — **Finley Peter Dunne**
- "The time for action is now. It's never too late to do something." — **Antoine de Saint-Exupéry**
- "Time will not slow down when something unpleasant lies ahead." — **Harry Potter**
- "Do not wait; the time will never be 'just right.' Start where you stand and work with whatever tools you may have at your command, and better tools will be found as you go along." — **George Herbert**
- "Time is a created thing. To say, 'I don't have time,' it is to say, 'I don't want to.'" — **Lao Tzu**
- "You build on failure. You use it as a steppingstone. Close the door on the past. You don't try to forget the mistakes, but you don't dwell on it. You don't let it have any of your energy, or any of your time, or any of your space." — **Johnny Cash**

"Concentrate on the things that matter in life. Money, fame, power and prestige are not on the top of the list."

- "If you don't have time to do it right, when will you have time to do it over?" — **John Wooden**
- "Any action is often better than no action, especially if you have been stuck in an unhappy situation for a long time. If it is a mistake, at least you learn something, in which case it's no longer a mistake. If you remain stuck, you learn nothing." — **Eckhart Tolle**
- "There are two types of patience. One is exercised in hard work and the other in idleness. Patience with hard work is the one that moves mountains. Patience in idleness moves nothing, not even cobwebs." — **Israelmore Ayivor**
- "Your success will be in direct proportion to how you spend your 'free' time." — **Mike Dunlap**
- "If you spend too much time thinking about a thing, you'll never get it done." — **Bruce Lee**

UNDERSTANDING AND USING TIME

- "You may delay, but time will not." — **Benjamin Franklin**
- "Your time is limited, so don't waste it living someone else's life. Don't be trapped by dogma — which is living with the results of other people's thinking. Don't let the noise of others' opinions drown out your own inner voice. And most importantly, have the courage to follow your heart and intuition. They somehow already know what you truly want to become. Everything else is secondary." — **Steve Jobs**
- "You will never find time for anything. If you want time, you must make it." — **Charles Buxton**
- "The way we spend our time defines who we are." — **Jonathan Estrin**
- "Remember, today is the tomorrow you worried about yesterday." — **Dale Carnegie**
- "This time, like all times, is a very good one, if we but know what to do with it." — **Ralph Waldo Emerson**

"Concentrate on the things that matter in life. Money, fame, power and prestige are not on the top of the list."

- "Don't let the fear of the time it will take to accomplish something stand in the way of your doing it. The time will pass anyway; we might just as well put that passing time to the best possible use." — **Earl Nightingale**
- "If you wait for the perfect moment when all is safe and assured, it may never arrive. Mountains will not be climbed, races won, or lasting happiness achieved." — **Maurice Chevalier**
- "Have regular hours for work and play; make each day both useful and pleasant and prove that you understand the worth of time by employing it well. Then youth will bring few regrets, and life will become a beautiful success." — **Louisa May Alcott**
- "Life isn't a matter of milestones, but of moments." — **Rose Kennedy**
- "It's surprising how much free time and productivity you gain when you lose the busyness in your mind." — **Brittany Burgunder**

"Concentrate on the things that matter in life. Money, fame, power and prestige are not on the top of the list."

- "No such thing as spare time, no such thing as free time, no such thing as downtime. All you got is a lifetime. Go." — **Henry Rollins**
- "I always live in the present. The future I can't know. The past I no longer have." — **Fernando Pessoa**
- "With technology and over-scheduling, we are forgetting to invest time in simple connective moments with others." — **Michelle Gielan**
- "For disappearing acts, it's hard to beat what happens to the eight hours supposedly left after eight of sleep and eight of work." — **Doug Larson**
- "They always say time changes things, but you actually have to change them yourself." — **Andy Warhol**
- "At the end of your life, you will never regret not having passed one more test, not winning one more verdict, or not closing one more deal. You will regret time not spent with a husband, a friend, a child, or a parent." — **Barbara Bush**

"Concentrate on the things that matter in life. Money, fame, power and prestige are not on the top of the list."

- "Don't live the same year 75 times and call it a life." — **Robin S. Sharma**
- "Time sometimes flies like a bird, sometimes crawls like a snail; but a man is happiest when he does not even notice whether it passes swiftly or slowly." — **Ivan Turgenev**
- "Half our time is spent trying to find something to do with the time we have rushed through life trying to save." — **Will Rogers**
- "Stop and take your time to notice things and make those things you notice matter." — **Cecelia Ahern**
- "People hurry so they can get to places faster, where they'd rather not be, so they can have more time to do things they'd rather not be doing." — **Peter Turla**
- "Free time is a terrible thing to waste. Read a book." — **E.A. Bucchianeri**
- "You can have it all. Just not all at once." — **Oprah Winfrey**

"Concentrate on the things that matter in life. Money, fame, power and prestige are not on the top of the list."

- "Free time was the most precious time when you should be doing what you loved or at least slowing down enough to remember what made your life worthwhile and happy." — **Amy Tan**
- "There's only one thing more precious than our time and that's who we spend it on." — **Leo Christopher**
- "Too often man handles life as he does the bad weather. He whiles away the time as he waits for it to stop." — **Alfred Polgar**
- "Time management is an oxymoron. Time is beyond our control, and the clock keeps ticking regardless of how we lead our lives. Priority management is the answer to maximizing the time we have." — **John C. Maxwell**
- "You've got to know what you want. This is central to acting on your intentions. When you know what you want, you realize that all there is left then is time management. You'll manage your time to achieve your goals

because you clearly know what you're trying to achieve in your life." — **Patch Adams**

- "Don't make the same decision twice. Spend time and thought to make a solid decision the first time so that you don't revisit the issue unnecessarily." — **Bill Gates**
- "Once you have mastered time, you will understand how true it is that most people overestimate what they can accomplish in a year — and underestimate what they can achieve in a decade!" — **Anthony Robbins**
- "Rearranging your day around when you have the most energy is one simple way to work smarter instead of just harder." — **Chris Bailey**
- "Time is the coin of your life. It is the only coin you have, and only you can determine how it will be spent. Be careful lest you let other people spend it for you." — **Carl Sandburg**
- "The most efficient way to live reasonably is every morning to make a plan of one's day

UNDERSTANDING AND USING TIME

and every night to examine the results obtained." — **Alexis Carrel**

- "A plan is what, a schedule is when. It takes both a plan and a schedule to get things done." — **Peter Turla**
- "He who every morning plans the transactions of that day and follows that plan carries a thread that will guide him through the labyrinth of the most busy life." — **Victor Hugo**
- "Until we can manage time, we can manage nothing else." — **Peter F. Drucker**
- "Time management requires self-discipline, self-mastery, and self-control more than anything else." — **Brian Tracy**
- "The butterfly counts not months but moments and has time enough." — **Rabindranath Tagore**
- "Multitasking is overrated — I'd rather do one thing well than many things badly. Quality supersedes quantity every time." — **Stewart Stafford**

- "The irony of multitasking is that it's exhausting: when you're doing two or three things simultaneously, you use more energy than the sum of energy required to do each task independently. You're also cheating yourself because you're not doing anything excellently." — **Twyla Tharp**
- "To do two things at once is to do neither." — **Publius Syrus**
- "Multitasking is like constantly pulling up a plant. This kind of constant shifting of your attention means that new ideas and concepts have no chance to take root and flourish." — **Barbara Oakley**
- "Multitasking divides your attention and leads to confusion and weakened focus." — **Deepak Chopra**
- "Multitasking arises out of distraction itself." — **Marilyn vos Savant**
- "You can do two things at once, but you can't focus effectively on two things at once." — **Gary Keller**

"Concentrate on the things that matter in life. Money, fame, power and prestige are not on the top of the list."

UNDERSTANDING AND USING TIME

- "One cannot manage too many affairs: like pumpkins in the water, one pops up while you try to hold down the other." — **Chinese Proverb**
- "Be like a postage stamp — stick to one thing until you get there." — **Josh Billings**
- "The shorter way to do many things is to only do one thing at a time." — **Wolfgang Amadeus Mozart**
- "Multitasking, when it comes to paying attention, is a myth." — **John Medina**
- "Procrastination is the art of keeping up with yesterday and avoiding today." — **Wayne Dyer**
- "We all sorely complain of the shortness of time and yet have much more than we know what to do with. Our lives are either spent in doing nothing at all, or in doing nothing to the purpose, or in doing nothing that we ought to do. We are always complaining that our days are few and acting as though there would be no end of them." — **Seneca**

"Concentrate on the things that matter in life. Money, fame, power and prestige are not on the top of the list."

- "Until you value yourself, you will not value your time. Until you value your time, you will not do anything with it." — **M. Scott Peck**
- "Concentrate all your thoughts upon the work in hand. The sun's rays do not burn until brought to a focus." — **Alexander Graham Bell**
- "Begin doing what you want to do now. We are not living in eternity. We have only this moment, sparkling like a star in our hand, and melting like a snowflake." — **Sir Francis Bacon**
- "Dare to be wise; begin! He who postpones the hour of living rightly is like the rustic who waits for the river to run out before he crosses." — **Horace**
- "Delay always breeds danger, and to protract a great design is often to ruin it." — **Miguel De Cervantes**
- "Nothing is so fatiguing as the eternal hanging on of an uncompleted task." — **William James**

UNDERSTANDING AND USING TIME

- "If you want to make good use of your time, you've got to know what's most important and then give it all you've got." — **Lee Iacocca**
- "Things which matter most must never be at the mercy of things which matter least." — **Johann Wolfgang von Goethe**
- "There is never enough time to do everything, but there is always enough time to do the most important thing." — **Brian Tracy**
- "The most important thing in life is knowing the most important things in life." — **David F. Jakielo**
- "We don't drift in good directions. We discipline and prioritize ourselves there." — **Andy Stanley**
- "You gotta make it a priority to make your priorities a priority." — **Richie Norton**
- "'I don't have time' is just saying it's not a priority." — **Naval Ravikant**
- "Don't say you don't have enough time. You have exactly the same number of hours

"Concentrate on the things that matter in life. Money, fame, power and prestige are not on the top of the list."

per day that were given to Helen Keller, Pasteur, Michelangelo, Mother Teresa, Leonardo da Vinci, Thomas Jefferson, and Albert Einstein."— **H. Jackson Brown Junior**

- "It is not enough to take steps which may someday lead to a goal; each step must be itself a goal and a step likewise." — **Johann Wolfgang von Goethe**

- "Don't be fooled by the calendar. There are only as many days in the year as you make use of. One man gets only a week's value out of a year while another man gets a full year's value out of a week." — **Charles Richards**

- "Ordinary people think merely of spending time. Great people think of using it." — **Anonymous**

- "Take care of the minutes and the hours will take care of themselves."— **Lord Chesterfield**

- "The main problem with this great obsession for saving time is very simple: you can't save time. You can only spend it. But

"Concentrate on the things that matter in life. Money, fame, power and prestige are not on the top of the list."

you can spend it wisely or foolishly." — **Benjamin Hoff**

- "One can only forget about time by making use of it." — **Charles Baudelaire**
- "As we speak, cruel time is fleeing. Seize the day, believing as little as possible in the morrow." — **Horace**
- "I must govern the clock, not be governed by it." — **Golda Meir**
- "Starting every year, before I booked anything, or agreed to any meetings or conferences, we'd sit down with my assistant, and we looked at our lives first. We planned that out first, and then what was left would be left for work." — **Michelle Obama**
- "One must work with time and not against it. "— **Ursula K. Le Guin**
- "Begin with the end in mind." — **Stephen Covey**
- "Give me six hours to chop down a tree and I will spend the first four sharpening the axe." — **Abraham Lincoln**

"Concentrate on the things that matter in life. Money, fame, power and prestige are not on the top of the list."

- "A goal without a plan is just a wish." — **Antoine de Saint-Exupéry**
- "Planning is bringing the future into the present so that you can do something about it now." — **Alan Lakein**
- "Lack of direction, not lack of time, is the problem. We all have twenty-four-hour days." — **Zig Ziglar**
- "The best time to start was last year. Failing that, today will do." — **Chris Guillebeau**
- "There is more to life than simply increasing its speed." — **Mahatma Gandhi**
- "Take your time. There's no rush to be good or renowned." — **Kathryn Budig**
- "If you're really looking for something in particular, it helps to take your time." — **Billy Gibbons**
- "When you take the small roads, you see the life that goes on there, this makes your own life larger." — **Elizabeth Berg**
- "You don't have to see the whole staircase, just take the first step." — **Martin Luther King, Jr.**

"Concentrate on the things that matter in life. Money, fame, power and prestige are not on the top of the list."

UNDERSTANDING AND USING TIME

- "Fast is fine, but accuracy is everything." — **Wyatt Earp**
- "The best thing about the future is that it comes one day at a time." — **Abraham Lincoln**
- "The important thing is to take your time and not get stressed." — **Diane von Furstenberg**
- "Haste in every business brings failures." — **Herodotus**
- "Perfection is attained by slow degrees; it requires the hand of time." — **Voltaire**
- "Regret for wasted time is more wasted time." — **Mason Cooley**
- "Time = life; therefore, waste your time and waste your life, or master your time and master your life." — **Alan Lakein**
- "People are frugal in guarding their personal property; but as soon as it comes to squandering time, they are most wasteful of the one thing in which it is right to be stingy." — **Seneca**

"Concentrate on the things that matter in life. Money, fame, power and prestige are not on the top of the list."

- "You must have been warned against letting the golden hours slip by, but some of them are golden only because we let them slip by." — **James Matthew Barrie**
- "Make use of time, let not advantage slip." — **William Shakespeare**
- "Realize that if you have time to whine and complain about something, then you have the time to do something about it." — **Anthony J. D'Angelo**
- "You can't have a better tomorrow if you are thinking about yesterday all the time." — **Charles F. Kettering**
- "Life is flying by. You don't have time to waste another minute being negative, offended, or bitter. If someone did you wrong, get over it and move forward." — **Joel Osteen**
- "Time stays long enough for those who use it." — **Leonardo Da Vinci**
- "Waste your money and you're only out of money but waste your time and you've lost a part of your life." — **Michael LeBoeuf**

"Concentrate on the things that matter in life. Money, fame, power and prestige are not on the top of the list."

- "A man who dares to waste one hour of time has not discovered the value of life." — **Charles Darwin**
- "It's not that we have a little time, but more that we waste a good deal of it." — **Seneca**
- "Time is the one thing that can never be retrieved. One may lose and regain a friend; one may lose and regain money; opportunity once spurned may come again; but the hours that are lost in idleness can never be brought back to be used in gainful pursuits."— **C.R. Lawton**
- "Defer no time, delays have dangerous ends." — **William Shakespeare**
- "Four things come not back, the spoken word, the sped arrow, time past, and the neglected opportunity." — **Arabian Proverb**
- "Time is really the only capital that any human being has, and the only thing he can't afford to lose." — **Thomas Edison**
- "Every second is of infinite value." — **Johann Wolfgang von Goethe**

"Concentrate on the things that matter in life. Money, fame, power and prestige are not on the top of the list."

- "An inch of time is an inch of gold, but you can't buy that inch of time with an inch of gold." — **Chinese Proverb**
- "Time is a gift that most of us take for granted. We get so caught up in the busyness of our daily lives that we rarely stop and take a serious look at how we're spending this gift." — **Cheryl Richardson**
- "My favorite things in life don't cost any money. It's really clear that the most precious resource we all have is time." — **Steve Jobs**
- "The two most powerful warriors are patience and time." — **Leo Tolstoy**
- "Time is the most valuable thing a man can spend." — **Theophrastus**
- "The common man is not concerned about the passage of time; the man of talent is driven by it." — **Schopenhauer**
- "Time moves slowly but passes quickly." — **Alice Walker**
- "All our sweetest hours fly fastest." — **Virgil**

"Concentrate on the things that matter in life. Money, fame, power and prestige are not on the top of the list."

UNDERSTANDING AND USING TIME

- "Time goes faster the more hollow it is." — **Carlos Ruiz Zafón**
- "I never think of the future. It comes soon enough." — **Albert Einstein**
- "Time flies over us, but leaves its shadow behind." — **Nathaniel Hawthorne**
- "The bad news is time flies. The good news is you're the pilot." — **Michael Altshuler**
- "The long unmeasured pulse of time moves everything. There is nothing hidden that it cannot bring to light, nothing once known that may not become unknown." — **Sophocles**
- "Time flies. It's up to you to be the navigator." — **Robert Orben**
- "The future is something which everyone reaches at the rate of sixty minutes an hour, whatever he does, whoever he is." — **C.S. Lewis**
- "Time is the most undefinable yet paradoxical of things; the past is gone, the future is not come, and the present becomes the past even while we attempt to define it,

"Concentrate on the things that matter in life. Money, fame, power and prestige are not on the top of the list."

UNDERSTANDING AND USING TIME

and, like the flash of lightning, at once exists and expires." — **Charles Caleb Colton**

- "Time and tide wait for no man, but time always stands still for a woman of 30." — **Robert Frost**
- "Never waste any time you can spend sleeping." — **Frank H. Knight**
- "Time is a great healer, but a poor beautician." — **Lucille S. Harper**
- "I'm going to stop putting things off, starting tomorrow!"— **Sam Levenson**
- "Time is money, especially when you're talking to a lawyer, or buying a commercial." — **Frank Dane**
- "So little time and so little to do." — **Oscar Levant**
- "Free time is death to the anxious and thank goodness I don't have any of it right now." — **Jon Stewart**
- "Enjoy life. There's plenty of time to be dead." — **Hans Christian Andersen**

"Concentrate on the things that matter in life. Money, fame, power and prestige are not on the top of the list."

- "To achieve great things, two things are needed; a plan, and not quite enough time." — **Leonard Bernstein**
- "I am definitely going to take a course on time management — just as soon as I can work it into my schedule." — **Louis Boone**
- "Punctuality is the thief of time." — **Oscar Wilde**
- "Time is a great teacher, but unfortunately, it kills all its pupils." — **Hector Berlioz**
- "To everything there is a season, and a time to every purpose under the heaven: A time to be born, and a time to die; a time to plant, and a time to pluck up that which is planted; A time to kill, and a time to heal; a time to break down, and a time to build up; A time to weep ., and a time to laugh; a time to mourn, and a time to dance; A time to cast away stones, and a time to gather stones together; a time to embrace, and a time to refrain from embracing; A time to get, and a time to lose; a time to keep, and a time to cast away; A time to tear and a time to sew;

"Concentrate on the things that matter in life. Money, fame, power and prestige are not on the top of the list."

UNDERSTANDING AND USING TIME

a time to keep silence, and a time to speak; A time to love, and a time to hate; a time of war, and a time of peace." – **Solomon; Ecclesiastes 3:1-11**

It is my hope that if you take the time to read these quotes at least one of them registers with you and helps you decide how to better manage the time you have or even think of it differently as you move forward through it. Even though all these quotes have some value, one quote that is not here is from a movie that I viewed a while ago and it really registered with me. I will share it with you now.

"Someone told me time was a predator that stalked us all our lives. I'd rather believe that time is a companion who goes with us on the journey and reminds us to cherish every moment because it will never come again." Patrick Stewart as Jean-Luc Picard (From the movie Star Trek Generations)

To me this quote embodies the fear and loathing of aging, but the hope and faith of time used wisely.

The other quote that directly registers with me is listed and it is from Solomon, mentioned in Bible as

"Concentrate on the things that matter in life. Money, fame, power and prestige are not on the top of the list."

the wisest man to ever live. I believe it also embodies some basic and important facts about time and that is in a nutshell there is time for all things and a season for all things. Proper use of our time allows us to enjoy every season of our lives to the ultimate extent. The basic tools listed in this book as well as the insights from others can serve as a starting point. The true process is knowing yourself and using that knowledge to progress forward and enjoy what life has to offer.

"Concentrate on the things that matter in life. Money, fame, power and prestige are not on the top of the list."

Chapter: 31

Concluding Thoughts

Benjamin Franklin is quoted as saying "In this world, nothing is as sure as death and taxes." I would take this quote a step further and say included in this surely is our march through time. Each of us is blessed with a start and end point and I have witnessed enough beginnings and endings to understand the blessing in the beginning and have seen some endings that were blessed and others that befuddled my mind.

The key whether your march is one day or 99 years, is to enjoy the journey as much as you can. This is not as hard as we make it and is usually driven by forces within our control. In Marvel and DC comics and movies universes they show what they call a multiverse, where different timelines exist based on each decision every person makes. There are currently close to 8 billion people on the planet earth. My guess is that we make no less than a hundred decisions each day at a minimum, some important, some not so much so. This would mean that in a single day no less than 800 billion different timelines would exist and so on and so forth. It is an interesting concept to think about. Being a religious man who feels and believes an omnipotent, omnipresent, omniscient God exists, I would say this is possible and he could absolutely allow it and cause it; but in the real world that most of us exist in, it is a straight line from beginning to end with a fixed start and end point. This entails most of us having to ponder a lot of what ifs related to decisions we made or did not make as we flow through time. What if I had invested in Apple when it started, what if I had said yes to him or her, what if I had followed my true passion? It is important not to allow ourselves to get caught up in the what ifs of our past. This can cause people to waste, or should I say, use a great bit of their time in useless reflection and wishful thinking about things in our past lives that cannot be changed. This requires us to accept where we are at any moment in time and if we are blessed with additional time, plan how we will utilize it not only for our personal benefit but for the benefit of every person we meet. This reminds me of a quote that says, "some people make a great

"The best exercise for your spiritual muscle Is to be on your knees In prayer"

impression on your life when they enter it, and other's make the best impression when they leave it." I pray that most people I meet feel that they are happy I was a part of their lives.

This realization brings us to the importance of time management. Every decision we make is, in essence, a management of our time—whether we invest it wisely, waste it, or ignore it. Time management is not only about deadlines and schedules; it is about aligning our choices with what truly matters to us. Each "yes" to one path is a "no" to countless others, and this is where reflection becomes essential. The choices that pull us toward growth, happiness, and fulfillment are what ultimately shape a meaningful life. Good time management is not simply about cramming in as much as possible; it is about making deliberate decisions, investing time where it enriches us, and focusing on what brings purpose and joy.

As we flow through time, mindful time management allows us to reduce regret and focus on the present moment. Instead of getting caught up in the past or lost in possibilities, we learn to make the best of our journey. The choices we make today, with the

"The best exercise for your spiritual muscle Is to be on your knees In prayer"

understanding that time is both finite and precious, can help us create a life that feels whole and fulfilling. In this way, time management becomes not just a strategy but a philosophy, enabling us to honor the certainty of time and live purposefully within its bounds.

"The best exercise for your spiritual muscle Is to be on your knees In prayer"

REFERENCES

https://www.beautyinthestorm.com/2015/01/unwanted.html?m=0

https://studyx.ai/questions/4ldxszy/activity-9-in-this-activity-your-knowledge-will-be-assessed-through-the-statements-that

https://feedyoursoulfitness.com/the-28-day-fitness-challenge/

https://focuskeeper.co/glossary/what-is-focus-improvement-strategies/

https://medium.com/@pranav.irl/hello-world-my-journey-begins-on-medium-0916f94f980c

https://versusarthritis.org/about-arthritis/managing-symptoms/diet/

https://www.kore-fit.com/post/the-relaxation-response-unlocking-the-power-of-calm

https://www.moonrkt.com/post/how-to-analyze-your-mistakes-and-improve-results-in-trading

https://www.katedaiglecounseling.com/2023/04/01/understanding-secure-attachment/

https://sizamoro.com/101-quotes-about-time/

https://history.fsu.edu/article/navigating-dissertation-and-career-reflections-journey-history-dave-lunger-phd-2024

https://www.linkedin.com/posts/neenamody-cprw-resume-consultant_change-thoughts-opportunities-activity-7292029043699322880-cI1V

https://timehackz.com/time-management-quotes/

https://www.lanredahunsi.com/top-30-quotes-on-time/

https://systemnibht.weebly.com/blog/thoughts-quotes

https://quotesjournal.com/time-quotes/

https://quotesjournal.com/time-quotes/

https://www.consultclarity.org/post/quotes-about-time

https://clockify.me/blog/fun/quotes-about-time-management/

https://clockify.me/blog/fun/quotes-about-time-management/

https://clockify.me/blog/fun/quotes-about-time-management/

https://www.managingcommunities.com/2009/05/25/steve-jobs-dont-be-trapped-by-dogma-which-is-living-with-the-results-of-other-peoples-thinking/

https://clockify.me/blog/fun/quotes-about-time-management/

https://www.consultclarity.org/post/quotes-about-time

https://timehackz.com/time-management-quotes/

https://clockify.me/blog/fun/quotes-about-time-management/

https://clockify.me/blog/fun/quotes-about-time-management/

https://clockify.me/blog/fun/quotes-about-time-management/

https://www.bisnis.com/read/20231107/638/1711906/109-kata-kata-bijak-bahasa-inggris-dan-artinya-penuh-makna-mendalam

https://clockify.me/blog/fun/quotes-about-time-management/

https://clockify.me/blog/fun/quotes-about-time-management/

https://clockify.me/blog/fun/quotes-about-time-management/

https://www.mos.ru/upload/documents/files/7820/Capitalideas25.pdf

https://www.bisnis.com/read/20231107/638/1711906/109-kata-kata-bijak-bahasa-inggris-dan-artinya-penuh-makna-mendalam

https://www.bisnis.com/read/20231107/638/1711906/109-kata-kata-bijak-bahasa-inggris-dan-artinya-penuh-makna-mendalam

https://www.bisnis.com/read/20231107/638/1711906/109-kata-kata-bijak-bahasa-inggris-dan-artinya-penuh-makna-mendalam

https://clockify.me/blog/fun/quotes-about-time-management/

https://clockify.me/blog/fun/quotes-about-time-management/

https://clockify.me/blog/fun/quotes-about-time-management/

https://clockify.me/blog/fun/quotes-about-time-management/

https://www.bisnis.com/read/20231107/638/1711906/109-kata-kata-bijak-bahasa-inggris-dan-artinya-penuh-makna-mendalam

https://www.bisnis.com/read/20231107/638/1711906/109-kata-kata-bijak-bahasa-inggris-dan-artinya-penuh-makna-mendalam

https://clockify.me/blog/fun/quotes-about-time-management/

https://clockify.me/blog/fun/quotes-about-time-management/

https://clockify.me/blog/fun/quotes-about-time-management/

https://clockify.me/blog/fun/quotes-about-time-management/

https://www.deliberatedirections.com/quotes-about-time/

https://clockify.me/blog/fun/quotes-about-time-management/

https://clockify.me/blog/fun/quotes-about-time-management/

https://www.calendar.com/blog/101-powerful-productivity-quotes-that-will-inspire-you-to-work-harder-smarter/

https://www.newsbreak.com/news/3341239017961-73-quotes-about-time-to-inspire-you-to-seize-every-moment

https://clockify.me/blog/fun/quotes-about-time-management/

https://www.consultclarity.org/post/quotes-about-observing-observation

https://quotesjournal.com/time-quotes/

https://www.calendar.com/blog/101-powerful-productivity-quotes-that-will-inspire-you-to-work-harder-smarter/

https://clockify.me/blog/fun/quotes-about-time-management/

https://clockify.me/blog/fun/quotes-about-time-management/

https://master-xuan.com/quotes-about-managing-time/

https://www.linkedin.com/pulse/brighter-days-unlocking-happiness-work-aleena-h-malik-duidc

https://clockify.me/blog/fun/quotes-about-time-management/

https://clockify.me/blog/fun/quotes-about-time-management/

https://quotesjournal.com/time-quotes/

https://clockify.me/blog/fun/quotes-about-time-management/

https://www.developgoodhabits.com/time-quotes/

https://clockify.me/blog/fun/quotes-about-time-management/

https://clockify.me/blog/fun/quotes-about-time-management/

https://clockify.me/blog/fun/quotes-about-time-management/

https://clockify.me/blog/fun/quotes-about-time-management/

https://clockify.me/blog/fun/quotes-about-time-management/

https://clockify.me/blog/fun/quotes-about-time-management/

https://kabar24.bisnis.com/read/20240808/243/1788678/50-kata-kata-bijak-kehidupan-berkelas-dan-simpel

https://www.kompas.com/tren/read/2023/05/13/160743865/pelipur-lara-gagal-paham-waktu

https://www.bisnis.com/read/20231107/638/1711906/109-kata-kata-bijak-bahasa-inggris-dan-artinya-penuh-makna-mendalam

https://hellofearless.com/blogs/blog/quotes-about-time

https://www.kompas.com/tren/read/2023/05/13/1607 43865/pelipur-lara-gagal-paham-waktu

https://www.bisnis.com/read/20231107/638/1711906/ 109-kata-kata-bijak-bahasa-inggris-dan-artinya-penuh-makna-mendalam

https://www.kompas.com/tren/read/2023/05/13/1607 43865/pelipur-lara-gagal-paham-waktu

https://www.andersfh.com/religious-poems

https://www.andersfh.com/religious-poems

https://www.andersfh.com/religious-poems

https://www.goodreads.com/quotes/891516-i-rather-believe-that-time-is-a-companion-who-goes

ABOUT THE AUTHOR

Dr. Von Waber Goodloe, MEA., ED.S, CLRP, SPHR, SHRM-SCP, SHRM-PMG is a distinguished management career leader embracing Labor Relations, Human Resources, Planning, State and Federal Government Reporting, Recruitment, Professional Development, Performance Management, Training, EEOC/ADA, Risk Management, Diversity, Compensation, Retirement, Security and Benefits of a Fortune 500 three service utility company, and has contributed to a large urban school system in the U.S. He is an expert in cross-functional team building, system analysis, strategic planning, leadership, communications, organizational development, and quality performance improvement.

In addition to all these qualities, he achieved them through earning a BA in Physics at Hampton University in 1983 and went on to earn his MS in Educational Administration (Magna cum laude) in 1994. To develop even more skills on this journey he earned an EDS (Education Specialist/Development) from Union University (Summa Cum Laude) in 2009. Because of his determination to enhance his career knowledge he continued his education with Union University and earned his EDD (Doctorate in Education) (Summa

Cum Laude) in 2011 and that is where he drew the line and decided he was now ready to pursue his dream careers.

Not only did he obtain these degrees, he earned the following Certifications: CLRP (Certified Labor Relations Professional) from the National Public Employer Labor Relations Association NPELRA, SPHR (Senior Professional Human Resources) HR Certification Institute, SHRM-SCP (Senior Certified Professional), SHRM-PMQ (People Manager Qualification) Society for Human Resource Management SHRM, Teacher/Administrator Certification (Tennessee) Administration, Mathematics, Physics, Advanced ICS Command and General Staff Complex Incidents (ICS-400) Tennessee Emergency Management Agency, Intermediate ICS Command for Expanding Incidents (ICS-300) Tennessee Emergency Management Agency.

Dr. Goodloe is a member of various respective Professional Associations including the Society for Human Resources Management, National Public Employers Labor Relations Association, Phi Delta Kappa International (Associate Member), Kappa Delta Pi – International Honor Society in Education. He is also a dedicated Community Service Volunteer as an Executive Sponsor of the United Way, Executive Sponsor of Junior Achievement, Executive Sponsor/Board Member of

Life Blood, American Diabetes Association, Executive Sponsor and a Top Achiever for the American Heart Association Heart Walk and lastly, he is an Executive Sponsor for Tour for the Cure. Dr. Goodloe resides in Memphis, Tennessee with his lovely wife Mrs. Sharon Goodloe and they have three beautiful adult children with one grandson.

Made in the USA
Coppell, TX
10 February 2026

71724671R00167